The Narcissist Gospel

Good News for the Prideful Heart

Daniel C. Jacobs

The Narcissist Gospel

Contents

Mortifying Pride

The Protestant Reformation is considered by many historians and scholars alike to have begun October 31st, 1517 when a fervid young German man by the name of Martin Luther nailed his Ninety-Five Theses to the door of the castle church in Wittenberg, Germany. Luther's actions set ablaze an entire generation of Christians who had become disillusioned with a number of doctrines and traditions within the Roman Catholic Church. Countless men & women risked their lives and freedoms to propel this movement which would reshape the topography of Christianity, and the world, forever. Men such as Philip Melanchthon, John Calvin, Ulrich Zwingli, John Bunyan and William Tyndale have left their thumbprints on the Protestant Church into modern times.

One such man whose impact can be seen in perpetuity is a man by the name of John Owen. Born in Oxfordshire, England in 1616, Owen lived a life of great accomplishment, yet simultaneously intense tribulation. Owen fathered eleven children with his first wife, Mary

Rooke, but tragically, he would have to bury not just his wife, but all eleven of their children.

At the age of 35, Owen was appointed to the prestigious position of Dean at Christ Church in Oxford. He also became one of the most published English authors of his time, not simply on theological topics, but also politics and economics.

Perhaps the most famous quote, which we will revisit a number of times throughout this book, comes from his popular work: The Mortification of Sin.

"Be killing sin, or sin will be killing you."

-   <u>John Owen</u>

In this work, Owen takes the position that Christians ought not to be simply sitting idly and addressing sin from a passive position as it arises. Rather, Christians should be actively seeking out the sins in their lives to put them to death. This concept, Owen garnered from the Apostle Paul in Colossians 3:5

"Put to death therefore what is earthly in you."

Paul doesn't simply tell us to "resist" what is earthly in us, but rather to execute our own earthly nature.

"For as by a man came death, by a man has come also the resurrection of the dead. For as in Adam all die, so also in Christ shall all be made alive."

- 1 Corinthians 15:21-22

Sin, both directly and also as an overarching theme, entered the world through one man: our father Adam. Before you and I were guilty of any sins of commission, we were already sinners by birth. Arguably, the first sin ever committed was not simply a minute act of disobedience, but rather, a deep dark longing within the heart of Adam to become like God.

"For God knows that when you eat of it your eyes will be opened, and you will be like God, knowing good and evil."

- Genesis 3:5

At this moment in history, pride became the patriarchal sin which would father a great multitude of abominations. Consider several of the commandments which God gave to Moses.

"You shall not commit adultery." (Ex. 20:14)

Adultery is not simply an isolated sin. The seventh commandment forbids adultery, yet the tenth commandment tells us that we are not to covet our neighbor's wife. It would not be farfetched to argue that in most cases of adultery, the precursor sin is coveting. A man sees how attractive his friend's wife is. Perhaps they hit it off at a friendly get-together and exchanged numbers to meet up for something as innocent as their children's soccer game. As time passes however, they begin to desire a more intimate relationship. The man sees how his friend neglects his wife's feelings in order to go golfing with his buddies. Then he considers the lack of intimacy between himself and his wife, and the thoughts begin to creep in: *"I deserve more."* Adultery wasn't the first area in which the man stumbled. Neither was coveting. The true root of his infidelity lays much deeper within. That foundational root is pride.

We can apply this same pattern to just about any sin under the sun and trace each and every one back to a man or woman's pride. When we lie to someone it is because we think we are above the truth, and the subsequent repercussions. When one steals something, it is because of an innate sense of entitlement to that object. We think we deserve more. The grass is greener in our neighbor's yard and that grass should be ours!

When our pride is permitted to wander unchecked, it lays the foundations for a host of sins, narcissism being no exception. Only by the power of the Holy Spirit through the Gospel can we who were once slaves to sin, begin to experience victory in our lives over our own pride, which will in turn trickle down to the more obvious, outward iniquities which we struggle so greatly to hide. My prayer is that as we look at various scriptural examples of pride, its sneaking subtleties, and how it affects various aspects of our lives, you would join me in the mortification of our pride that we might flourish in humility through the work of the Holy Spirit in our hearts and minds.

Chapter 1

The Unseen Battle

One name that has commanded worldwide attention for over two millennia, unto the present, is that of The Roman Empire. Although not the largest empire in world history by any means, Rome had a certain "je ne sais quoi" that has dare I say, "conquered" the literary and cinematic world throughout the current era. Films such as Gladiator and The Eagle, along with William Shakespeare's theatrical "Julius Caesar" have garnered millions of viewers and the numbers are ever increasing.

At the height of its success, in 117 A.D. under Emperor Trajan, The Roman Empire controlled nearly 2 million square miles of territory across Western Europe and throughout the Middle East. Rome controlled every inch of coastline along the Mediterranean Sea, including a large portion of North Africa, which is apparent in the story of Phillip and the Ethiopian Eunuch from Acts 8. The fame of various Roman emperors has endured into modern times through literature and Hollywood such as: Marcus Aurelius, Commodus, Titus, Nero, and the aforementioned Julius Caesar. However, one name of particular interest to us is that of Emperor Caligula.

Ascending the throne in 37 A.D. at the age of 24, Caligula was quite possibly the most atrocious of rulers that the empire ever conceived, aside from possibly Nero who illuminated the streets of Rome with Christians as human torches. Caligula was well known for his creativity when it came to punishing those who infringed upon Roman law, or simply his own massively inflated ego. The historian Seneca recorded an instance in which Caligula ordered a nobleman to watch as his own son was executed and then forced him to sit by his side at a banquet following the execution. Caligula also reportedly would escort many of the married female guests of his palace to show them his collection of expensive glassware, only to "have his way" with them, and then announce this later on to everyone in attendance at the palace, including their husbands. That doesn't even factor in whether or not it was a consensual encounter.

Life for Emperor Caligula came to a head when his own bodyguards had finally grown tired of his antics and, in pure John Wilkes Booth fashion, stabbed him in the theatre. As Caligula fell to the ground, members of his court and the senate began to savagely seize their moment of revenge. The scene is quite reminiscent of the execution of Muammar Gaddafi of Libya in 2011, in which his body was tied to the front of a car and paraded through the streets for the angry mob to violate and spit upon.

This example of Emperor Caligula may seem at first to be quite exaggeratory in nature. Truthfully, this isn't a very tangible figure that is relatable to those of us in 21st century first world nations. The portrait that we derive from this clearly deranged individual, however, is that of unbridled, unrepentant pride. You may be thinking, "I'm sure the guy had an ego, but there's a lot more going on here than just pride," and you'd be correct. What we see however, is most often, nothing more than the symptoms of a much more sinister underlying disease.

When speaking to his disciples about false prophets, Jesus said these words:

"You will recognize them by their fruits. Are grapes gathered from thornbushes, or figs from thistles? So,

every healthy tree bears good fruit, but the diseased tree bears bad fruit. A healthy tree cannot bear bad fruit, nor can a diseased tree bear good fruit. Every tree that does not bear good fruit is cut down and thrown into the fire. Thus you will recognize them by their fruits."

– Matthew 7:16-20

These words draw an interesting parallel to those of Jesus' sermon in John 15:

"I am the true vine, and my Father is the vinedresser. Every branch in me that does not bear fruit he takes away, and every branch that does bear fruit he prunes, that it may bear more fruit. Already you are clean because of the word that I have spoken to you. Abide in me, and I in you. As the branch cannot bear fruit by itself, unless it abides in the vine, neither can you, unless you abide in me. I am the vine; you are the branches. Whoever abides in me and I in him, he it is that bears much fruit, for apart from me you can do nothing. If anyone does not abide in me he is thrown away like a branch and withers; and the branches are gathered, thrown into the fire, and burned."

- John 15:1-6

Indubitably, the key to understanding the source of these fruits is found here in verse four.

"Abide in me, and I in you. As the branch cannot bear fruit by itself, unless it abides in the vine, neither can you, unless you abide in me."

If we abide in Christ, we will produce the fruits of godliness. However, if we abide elsewhere, we will bear the rotten produce of our flesh. Caligula was a prime example of a deeply diseased tree whose rancid stench is still beheld 2,000 years later in our history books. What accentuates his wretchedness to the degree which we see is that he was the totalitarian ruler of the largest empire in the contemporary world. There were no checks or balances on his power, therefore his massive character flaws were left to snowball, resulting in one of history's greatest monsters. What then, was the root of Caligula's horrendous behavior? The obvious Sunday school answer is sin, and that is certainly correct. Perhaps the precise answer, however, boils down to one particular sin: Pride.

If we take a proverbial walk in the garden, I believe we'll all arrive at this same conclusion. Consider what satan says to Eve at the fall in Genesis 3:

"For God knows that when you eat of it your eyes will be opened, and you will be like God..."

- Genesis 3:5

Sin finds its initial conception within the heart of man the moment that Adam thought he deserved something more than God had provided. When Eve thought "I can be LIKE GOD," her and Adam made mankind's premiere attempt to usurp the power and position that belongs solely to the one who spoke everything into existence. In some way, each of us has made the same conscious choice to try and become our own counterfeit deity. Each and every time we choose sin over righteousness, we are saying "God, I know better than you." We attempt to claim sovereignty over our own lives and make ourselves lords over our own tiny kingdoms. Since the fall in Genesis 3, human civilization has been constructing empires & kingdoms in an attempt to glorify ourselves. In the midst of this unrelenting strife, we have all grown into little narcissists.

If you've picked up this book, it's possible that you have a family member or friend in mind that is displaying various attributes of narcissistic personality disorder. Perhaps you have grown up in a home with a narcissistic parent or are living with a spouse who is hitting all the textbook markers. As we discuss what scripture says in regard to narcissism, let me encourage you to take an introspective look at your own heart and thought processes. Often, the sins we observe in another can be quite revealing of our own iniquities if we pursue a greater level of self-awareness through the power of the Holy Spirit.

The puritan pastor, John Owen, once said:

"Be killing sin, or sin will be killing you."

The major source of this timeless quote comes from the Apostle Paul's letter to the church in Colossae:

"Put to death, therefore, what is earthly in you…"

– Colossians 3:5

The major theme we as believers can garner here from the Apostle Paul and John Owen is that we must be **active** in waging war against our fleshly tendencies. We cannot sit by passively watching life occur and expect to grow into the image of Christ. The Christian life is not idle. With that being said, we also need to realize that we are not the ones fighting and winning these internal struggles. Notice that Jesus didn't tell his disciples in John 15 that if they really dig in and try harder, then they'll bear good fruit. On the contrary, He says:

"Abide in me and I in you…" (v. 4)

and,

"For apart from me you can do nothing." (v. 5)

2 Chronicles 20 gives us a tangible example of this concept. The Moabites, Ammonites, and Meunites had rallied together to come against the nation of Judah. At that time, Jehoshaphat is King of Judah and when he sees the hordes of the other kingdoms coming against him, he is terrified.

"Then Jehoshaphat was afraid and set his face to seek the Lord, and proclaimed a fast throughout all Judah."

Notice that Jehoshaphat's response to this impending doom isn't to devise some sort of plan to try and flank the Ammonites from the rear or set an ambush for the Moabites. Rather, scripture says he sought the Lord and proclaimed a fast. From an earthly perspective, proclaiming a fast was a truly astern thing to do prior to a forthcoming battle. Starving your own armies so that they are malnourished and weak before a fight is certainly not in your best interests. Yet, King Jehoshaphat displays that his faith was not in the armies of Judah or the walls of his cities but rather in the Lord.

"And he said, "Listen, all Judah and inhabitants of Jerusalem and King Jehoshaphat: Thus says the Lord to you, 'Do not be afraid and do not be dismayed at this great horde, for the battle is not yours but God's.'"

- 2 Chronicles 20:15

Jehoshaphat trusted that Yahweh, the God of Israel, would go to war on his behalf if he trusted in Him to deliver the people of Judah.

"You will not need to fight in this battle. Stand firm, hold your position, and see the salvation of the Lord on your behalf, O Judah and Jerusalem.' Do not be afraid and do not be dismayed. Tomorrow go out against them, and the Lord will be with you."

- 2 Chronicles 20:17

Later in chapter 20, we see that the armies of Judah didn't have to lift a finger. The Lord caused the armies that had come against them to turn and fight one another. The inhabitants of Judah simply had to go down to the camps of the armies that were lying dead on the battlefield and collect the spoils of battle. Verse 25 tells us that they were there three days plundering the camps of their enemies.

As we go to war against the sin of pride in our own hearts, it would behoove us to keep this story in the forefront of our minds, lest we forget that the battle is not ours but the Lord's. But we must show up for the fight.

Chapter 2

Defining Narcissism

"Pride goes before destruction, and a haughty spirit before a fall."
Proverbs 16:18

Oxford Languages defines the word "narcissist" as "a person who has an excessive interest in or <u>admiration</u> of themselves."

It doesn't take most of us long to think of someone we know, or may simply know of, that fits this definition quite well. Whether it be a parent, spouse, friend, colleague, or a well-known celebrity, we don't have to reach very far to find one. My father fit the bill to a concerning degree. There are ways in which he was a great father that I can't, and don't wish to take away from him. However, if ever there were a man whose photograph belonged in the dictionary next to the word narcissist, it was him. As a matter of fact, I can think of three different photographs that he had printed of himself that were posted up in his office at home. The first was of him jumping waves on his old jet ski from when I was a kid. The second, of him with no shirt on next to my sister before her junior prom. And the third was him posing shirtless while playing beach volleyball. Initially, I thought nothing of these. I saw them as him merely reliving good times from his younger years. However, as the years went by and I watched these three photos being peddled to anyone that visited my parent's home, I started to see the hidden picture a bit more clearly.

I began to take note of how every conversation somehow refocused on him, regardless of the initial subject. I can recall having to stop him from constantly interrupting whenever I was trying to communicate something and needed him to listen. We would regularly get into spiritual or theological discussions and rarely did we agree. He was one of those interesting folks that was a self-proclaimed "prophet." Now, I do believe in the gift of prophecy, as I am by no means a cessationist. However, my father and I's perspective on how that gift fleshed out in the modern-day church was quite different.

Typically, in christian families, the father is more conservative and hopes to pass on the same traditional biblical values to his children. In my family, however, this was quite the opposite. My father rarely dusted off his Bible though he prayed all the time. He always said that God spoke to him in a special way. The problem was that this "special revelation" often wasn't cohesive with what we find in God's Word. Furthermore, if you didn't agree with him, or dared to challenge what he believed God had told him, then you were being "controlled by the evil one" and outside of God's will. Honestly, when I was younger I really believed the majority of what he said the Lord had shown him.

Fortunately, the Lord placed me with a high school small group leader, by the name of Tim, who for some reason or another felt a strong burden to help me understand how crucial it is that we treat God's Word with great care in our studies. When we first met, I used scripture carelessly to make it say whatever I wanted. It's quite easy really, to take verses and passages out of context and draw inaccurate, or downright heretical conclusions based more in what we want to believe about God, as opposed to what the Bible actually says about Him. This act in itself is actually creating a false god. Tim Keller stated it this way:

"If your god never disagrees with you, you might just be worshipping an idealized version of yourself."

Read that again.

Creating a false god doesn't require golden statues or little wooden figures. It often looks a lot more like our own reflection in a mirror.

As previously stated, my small group leader, Tim, was absolutely instrumental in the massive paradigm shift that the Lord had in store for me. Around this time our church had a high school boys trip planned to Cedar Point which was at the time the number one ranked roller coaster park in the world. And I really didn't want to go. I actually love rollercoasters, but for whatever reason, I really didn't want to go on that trip. Tim, however, felt very strongly that the Holy Spirit wanted me to go on this trip. He pressed and pressed and even called my mother about it, who eventually made sure that I was on the bus.

On our way home (a twenty-two-hour drive), late at night, I ended up sitting in the front passenger seat of the church van talking with Tim about "hermeneutics." If you're unfamiliar with the term, it essentially refers to the proper ways and processes to study scripture so that we learn what God wanted us to learn when He initially composed scripture through its various authors. Now my father referred to this man as a "Pharisee" and didn't like that I was being influenced by him one bit. Honestly, at the time, I really wished Tim would just leave me alone and let me read my Bible the way I wanted to read it. In hindsight however, there are few people whose influence I'm more thankful for in my life as a young man. That night my perspective began to slowly shift until I came to the place where I sought the Lord for what He says about himself in His Word, as opposed to creating a god in my own likeness, who agreed with my every opinion and feeling.

This opened up an entirely new world, and I began studying Systematic Theology, and reading all sorts of books about the attributes of God. Some of the information was easy to digest, however there were definitely some harder pills to swallow, especially after having been raised with very loose and liberal theology.

Some kids give their parents a heart-attack when they get pregnant out of wedlock. Others, when they come out of the closet regarding their sexual orientation. I'm quite certain however, that I nearly gave my father a stroke the day I told him I was being ordained as a Southern-Baptist deacon. I believe the words he said were:

"I don't know how *my son* of all people, ended up at a Southern-Baptist church, let alone as a deacon!"

As I formerly mentioned, every subject and conversation somehow made its way back to revolving around him. Once again, much like in the context of Emperor Caligula, we're talking about a pretty exaggerated case.

Yet, some of these unhealthy habits, I realized in my late twenties, I had picked up on. Having become an avid weightlifter after graduating high school, I could hardly pass by a mirror without stopping to see how I looked. How did the shirt I was wearing make my arms look? How were my lats looking after that back workout? The realization of this was downright terrifying. Having seen the affects of this manner of thinking throughout my childhood and into adulthood from my own father, I certainly didn't want to emulate those characteristics.

Depravity

If you would like a prayer that you can take to the bank… one that you can count on being answered swiftly and with the transparency of a glass of distilled water, ask God to reveal the sin of your heart and to sanctify you in his image. If you're unfamiliar with the term "sanctification," the simplest way to think of it is like an artist making a copy of a masterpiece. While it will never truly be the exact image of the original artwork, it will little by little turn a blank canvas into something admirers all around the globe will recognize instantly. Whether that be the Mona Lisa by Leonardo DaVinci, The Starry Night by Van Gogh, or The Creation of Adam by Michelangelo. In our case, we as Christians are being made into the image of Jesus throughout our walk with him, through the work of the Holy Spirit in us. He (the Holy Spirit) is in fact the one who reveals to us the wretchedness of our own hearts and minds. Moreover, He is the one who does this miraculous work of sanctification on our dusty, broken, and stained canvases.

In his "Doctrines of Grace" John Calvin taught several theological perspectives that Protestants have divided on for centuries. One however, that is much less divisive is the doctrine of Total Depravity. This idea is that man, to his core, has been corrupted by sin. We are morally depraved and utterly sinful. Were it not for the work of God in our lives, we would continue down this path of depravity until we too were just like Emperor Caligula. The Apostle Paul took particular care to be sure that we would be aware of this fact about our nature when writing Romans 3:

"None is righteous, no, not one; No one understands; No one seeks for God. All have turned aside; together they

have become worthless; No one does good, not even one.”

> *– Romans 3:10-12*

“For all have sinned and fallen short of the glory of God.”

> *– Romans 3:23*

If you think Paul was being a bit coarse in his assessment of our brokenness, just wait until you see what Jesus had to say during the sermon on the mount when He was teaching His followers to ask and it will be given. We tend to think of that phrase with great comfort and maybe even a sigh of relief. However, Jesus slipped a rather large and foundational truth into this comforting passage.

*“Ask, and it will be given to you; seek, and you will find; knock, and it will be opened to you. For everyone who asks receives, and the one who seeks finds, and to the one who knocks it will be opened. Or which one of you, if his son asks him for bread, will give him a stone? Or if he asks for a fish, will give him a serpent? **If you then, who are evil**, know how to give good gifts to your children, how much more will your Father who is in heaven give good things to those who ask him!”*

- *Matthew 7:7-11*

"Hold on Jesus! I realize that I'm a sinner… but evil?!"

In order for us to have a right understanding of the Gospel, we must first comprehend our own brokenness and need for a savior. Paul says we are worthless, no good sinners. Jesus says we are evil. Self-awareness is a quality most often absent in our world today, whether Christian or secular (As a side note: nothing is secular to the Lord. It is all His anyways). When we become aware of our sinfulness, we are able to take the first step towards sanctification. It's no wonder the devil works so hard to keep us blinded to our pride. When we fail to recognize our pride and therefore do not address it with the Holy Spirit, our pride then remains unbridled and allowed to roam freely, producing a host of other sins in our lives. Paul speaks of our former blindness in this way:

"In their case the god of this world has blinded the minds of the unbelievers, to keep them from seeing the light of the gospel of the glory of Christ, who is the image of God."

When Paul says, "god of this world," he is not speaking of God, but rather the devil. His modus operandi is deception, and his greatest work is to keep us from realizing our own bondage to sin. But God has the power to open the eyes of our hearts to the Gospel.

"...having the eyes of your hearts enlightened, that you may know what is the hope to which he has called you, what are the riches of his glorious inheritance in the saints, and what is the immeasurable greatness of his power toward us who believe, according to the working of his great might that he worked in Christ when he raised him from the dead and seated him at his right hand in the heavenly places, far above all rule and authority and power and dominion, and above every name that is named, not only in this age but also in the one to come."

- *Ephesians 1:18-21*

The Internal Struggle

What then does the sin of pride look like deep down? It's no difficult task to look at men like Caligula, or Commodus and hear the deafening shouts of a major internal battle with pride. But what about you? What about me?

We live in a world so full of blatant narcissism that we in many respects have grown numb to such disillusionment. Social media has made this painfully apparent. Between product influencers, instagram models and others who've simply made their living by building a large following with one form of niche content or another, we are inundated with self-obsession to a degree which the world has never before known. In full disclosure, I stopped writing for years because of this very issue at hand. I'd always enjoyed writing since I became a believer. Early on in my new life as a Christian I began writing blog posts on the Gospel. One day however, after praying that the Lord would reveal my own sin to me and sanctify me, I became painfully aware of a major issue in my own heart. I had grown far to attached to the feedback I got from friends who read my posts. I felt as if I had truly written something special that the world needed to hear. God had given *me*, a special word.

At this point in life, I cringe to even think about that because it was such a self-centered abuse of the Gospel. What an awful way to profane the blood of

Jesus! Using what he did on the cross to feed my own pride. This is one of those learned traits I picked up from growing up with a narcissistic father who did that very thing. In all reality, it is likely more appropriate to attribute such thinking to our corrupted flesh, or as the New International Version refers to it: our "sinful nature." When the Holy Spirit revealed this disgusting fact to me, I stopped writing altogether for years; probably over a decade.

We must strive to maintain a keen awareness of the focus of our heart. As we've already discussed, idolatry is far more prevalent than we give it credit for. We have TV series' such as "American Idol." Reality shows that glorify particular lifestyles, designed to make viewers thirst for a taste of. The best modern example that comes to mind would be the award-winning series Yellowstone. This show ought to be key study material for every marketing student in America, because Taylor Sheridan successfully made millions of Americans feel like they were a part of this cowboy mafia. While I'm not a big fan of much of the content, I have to give a hand to the writers and producers for the way they were able to captivate their audience.

Are we so affectionately captivated by the Lord though? John Piper once said, "Man was made for mountains, not mirrors." How terrible a thing it is that we so easily lose ourselves in our own image and reputation, that we miss the beauty of the infinite God right in front of us. This would be like taking a trip to Mt. Zion National Park, hiking up the mountain, and when you sit to take a break, you pull out your phone to take a selfie with nothing but the unfocused dirt in the background. Then you spend the next few minutes putting together a social media post telling your friends what you're doing and where you're at. Yet, if you'd just turn the camera around, you could share the vast beauty of God's handiwork and enjoy it yourself. This is exactly what we do in ministry when we use our position to take some of the glory and attention for ourselves, rather than pointing the full attention to Christ, and saying "Not to us, oh Lord, but to your name be the glory!" (Psalm 115:1) Often this isn't even a fully conscious choice either. Rather, subconsciously we are saying:

> "Hear how good of a voice I have?"

> "See how cool of a pastor I am?"

> "Cool guitar solo, right?"

> "See how I raise my hands and squint my eyes in worship? It's because I'm so spiritual."

While most of us would never actually verbalize those statements, I do believe we can easily fall into having them as an underlying note that slowly begins to chisel a little golden image of ourselves to put up in a corner of our temple.

James 4:6 says, *"God opposes the proud but gives grace to the humble."*

Now, I don't know about you, but being in opposition to Almighty God is certainly not an item on my to-do list. As a matter of fact, a light perusing of the Old Testament will give one a great insight into what it looks like to be an opponent of the Lord. This is one of the reasons that the enemy promotes this idea that the Old Testament is somehow obsolete for us as Christians now. While we no longer remain under the law, bound by the Mosaic Covenant, we love and serve the same God who wrote the law and delivered it to Moses for the people of Israel. The same God who destroyed Sodom & Gomorrah with fire also offered Himself in our place on the cross. Jesus himself spoke quite extensively about judgement on sin. We as believers need not fear punishment any longer because the blood of Christ has atoned for all time, our every sin, however, we also ought to have a reverence for our Father so that when we

recognize sin in our hearts, we repent at once and run the
other direction.

In this new era of technology and social media,
we have grown more fixated on ourselves than ever
before. With the simple swipe of a finger, we have a
screen staring back at us with our own image. Our world
is one big house of mirrors. It's time we take hold of
these mirrors and throw them to the ground. Let the glass
that once held our attention captive lose its luster and
free us to look up to the mountainous glory of God.

In John 3, we see a conversation between John
the Baptist and one of his disciples who is concerned that
all the crowds are leaving them and going to follow
Jesus. When confronted about this by his disciple, John
responds with a statement that summarizes the entire aim
of this book better than anything I could personally
muster:

"He must increase, but I must decrease." (John 3:30)

Repentance

*"Or do you suppose it is to no purpose that the Scripture
says, "He yearns jealously over the spirit that he has
made to dwell in us"? But he gives more grace.
Therefore it says, "God opposes the proud but gives*

Depending on how you look at it, I believe we're either all born as little narcissists, or none of us are. Honestly, both assertions have some underlying credibility. Regardless of one's foundational perspectives on this, I don't believe that anyone is born with the clinical diagnosis of narcissistic personality disorder. Narcissism, on the other hand, is the long-term product of years of unchecked and unrepentant pride. Each of us has the capacity to fall into this hole like Alice in Wonderland. It is so crucial that we take inventory of our own hearts and thought processes to see what fruits we as believers are producing. One thing my wife and I regularly discuss is how modern medicine often treats the symptoms of a disease rather than the cause. When we look introspectively at ourselves, with the help of the Holy Spirit, we can begin to see what truly is going on in our own hearts, and God can then treat the underlying sin responsible for the rotten fruit we so desperately try to hide. I believe the sin that lies at the root of most of our personality faults & disorders is pride.

"Ones Pride will bring him low, but he who is lowly in spirit will obtain honor."

-        *Proverbs 29:23*

The contrast displayed here in this verse is pure gold. What Solomon is essentially saying here is this: You **will** be made low one way or another. You can humble yourself or God can humble you, but if you humble yourself, you will receive honor.

We see a similar theme in regard to eschatology in the Apostle Paul's letter to the church in Philippi:

"Therefore, God also highly exalted Him, and bestowed on Him the name which is above every name, so that at the name of Jesus every knee will bow, of those who are in heaven and on earth and under the earth, and that every tongue will confess that Jesus Christ is Lord, to the glory of God the Father."

-        *Philippians 2:9-11*

Notice how Paul doesn't say that every believer's knee will bow, or that every Christian's tongue will confess that Jesus is Lord. On the contrary he makes the definitive statement that **every** knee will bow, and **every** tongue confess that Jesus Christ is Lord to the glory of God the Father. At that moment in time, when the world is before the King of Kings and Lord of Lords, none of us will be able to resist His glory. This is such an incredible picture of the greatness and majesty of our Lord.

As every knee is bowed, so every heart will be humbled before the Living God. It would greatly behoove us, as believers, to start this process of humility now.

At the end of my father's life, he was humbled. It wasn't voluntarily, but God brought him low. Likewise, Caligula was brutally murdered by his own bodyguards and court members. Consider for a moment other examples throughout history. Julius Caesar was murdered by around 40 Roman Senators and his own best friend Brutus. Napoleon Bonaparte died in exile. Alexander the Great died from a mosquito bite.

No matter what level of greatness we each attain throughout our relatively short lives: We all die. Moreover, The Lord has a way of humbling each of us if we refuse to do so ourselves. That is the real purpose behind this book. This is not a psychology book on narcissism. It's not a self-help book. My purpose in writing this was to equip believers with the biblical tools to make war on the sin of pride. If we're ever going to begin claiming victory over the vast array of sins we each face in our day to day lives, we must first learn to address the trojan horse that lies within each of us.

Chapter 3

A Note About the Author (Of Salvation)

"And he is before all things, and in him all things hold together."
Colossians 1:17

As the father of three, I have come to the understanding that children are quite possibly God's greatest sanctifiers. My two oldest are both exceptionally strong-willed and have been from quite early ages. My oldest, shortly after his first birthday began to test where all of the boundaries were, and what their consequences were. "Was Dad serious when he said not to throw my fork on the ground? How about this time?"

We have tried all sorts of different disciplinary techniques on each of them, however, I've found nothing creates positive change quite like reaching the heart of your child. Honestly, I can't take credit for figuring that out either. It was my wife who concluded through her own prayers and studies that sometimes a big emotional impulse from one of our little ones didn't need to be met with the full force of the paternal gestapo. Sometimes begging the question, "Do you need a hug?" created far greater results than my drill sergeant techniques. Though from time to time, I do have to let my inner Lee Ermey out to restore order. I have quite a few comical stories, but I'll save those for the chapter on Narcissism in Parenting.

What then, does all of this have to do with pride? Well, its really about addressing our sins starting at the heart. We can treat the symptoms of our ailments all we want but we won't be getting any better that way. On the other hand, we can simply learn to live with them and grow numb to their constant antagonizing presence. However, there remains a third and supremely better option: When we treat the underlying cause of our character defects, they will begin to dissipate on their own. I'm preaching to myself here.

To get a good grasp on this concept, we must first start at the source… the Author of Life. If we are to understand how we were created to live and function, we must first come to some level of understanding of who God is. Not that we'll ever comprehend Him in His entirety, for if that were the case, He wouldn't be a very great God. So then we ask, who is God? What is He? What are His attributes? There have been countless books written on these subjects. Three that I highly recommend if you want to understand more about God's attributes are:

1.) The Attributes of God, by Arthur Pink
2.) Knowing God, by J.I. Packer
3.) The Knowledge of The Hole, by A.W. Tozer

As a preface to the subject, I think we ought to ask ourselves "Why is it important that we think rightly of God?" Tozer says, "What comes to our minds when we think about God is the most important thing about us." Consider for a moment that someone is spreading false rumors about you. Obviously, you're going to be upset upon hearing this. Regardless of how grand or inconsequential the issue may be, it is still a lie about you as a person. Genesis 1:27 tells us that God created man and woman in His image. We were created to reflect the very nature and characteristics of God Almighty! Therefore, as we are offended by erroneous statements about ourselves, so God is offended when we speak of Him incorrectly. I would argue that when we speak incorrectly of God, or even think about Him in a fallacious manner, we are breaking the first three of the Ten Commandments.

First, "You shall have no other gods before me."

Second, "You shall not make any graven images of anything in heaven or on earth."

And Third, "You shall not take the name of the Lord your God in vain."

When we think falsely of God, we are in essence, creating a false god. Subsequently, we devise a false image of the one we're supposed to be worshipping, and in turn attribute all of this to the Lord. This is why theology is so important!

Tozer once wrote:

"Let us beware lest we in our pride accept the erroneous notion that idolatry consists only in kneeling before visible objects of adoration, and that civilized peoples are therefore free from it. The essence of idolatry is the entertainment of thoughts about God that are unworthy of Him."

The fruit we see in our lives are the produce of whatever is inside of us. When we see an orange tree producing shriveled, spotted oranges, we instantly know that there is something wrong with the tree. We can pick off all of the diseased oranges, but we will continue to reap diseased oranges until we treat the disease that has infected the tree. If we leave the tree untreated, the disease will eventually take over and kill the whole tree. This is the essence of Narcissism; it is the product of one never treating the diseased root of pride in their heart. When we refuse to repent of sin, that sin is allowed to continue to grow & spread like a virus until it has killed its host. What then is our antidote? The answer is quite simple, albeit, often difficult for one to accept or grasp. It is the Gospel. If we get transparent with ourselves for a moment and take an authentic look at our own sinfulness in light of the One True Holy God, we are bound to see our pride wilt like a flower in the midday sun. The Apostle Paul called this renewing our minds.

"I appeal to you therefore brothers, by the mercies of God, to offer your bodies as a living sacrifice, holy and acceptable to God, which is your spiritual act of worship. Do not be conformed to this world, but be transformed by the renewing of your mind, that by testing you may discern what is the will of God, what is good and acceptable and perfect."

- *Romans 12:1-2*

Paul is essentially saying "Live a holy life. Sacrifice your wants and desires. But do it by first letting the Holy Spirit change your mind."

We must let the Gospel change the way we think. When the Word of God penetrates out hearts and convicts us of sin, we don't simply repent for fear of punishment. Rather, we repent out of love for our savior and King. Paul says in Romans 2:4 that the Kindness of God leads us to repentance. When we dwell on our father's kindness, obedience becomes much more natural.

When I was a teenager, I lived primarily with my mother, as my father had divorced and remarried when I was in middle school. There was a period of time where I definitely acted out on the unstable home situation that

I was learning to cope with. And thankfully, it was in this rough period of time where the Lord got ahold of my heart and I began to follow Him. I began to realize the stability my mother worked so hard to provide for me on a public-school teacher's salary as a single mother. She even went back to school and got her master's degree during this time. I look back now and realize that my mother was truly super-woman! In all of this growth as a young man both naturally and now spiritually, my mother and I grew very close.

I can recall some friends in high school asking me to go do something with them that I knew with certainty I was not allowed to do, and I said just that. They replied: "Just don't tell you mom." Had my mother not worked so hard to build the relationship we had, I very well may have listened to my friends and done what I knew I wasn't permitted to do, but the thought of my choices disappointing her was a much bigger deal to me than what they thought. I try to keep this principle in mind as I raise my own children.

It wasn't the rod of iron that my mother ruled with, though that reality certainly didn't escape me! It was her kindness that led me to choosing a higher road. As we immerse ourselves in the Gospel, our minds are renewed in the kindness of God and our lives are thus transformed little by little into the image of God as we were originally intended to reflect. Charles Spurgeon once wrote:

"Would you lose your sorrow? Would you drown your cares? Then go, plunge yourself in the Godhead's deepest sea; be lost in his immensity; and you shall come forth as from a couch of rest, refreshed and invigorated. I know nothing which can so comfort the soul; so calm the swelling billows of sorrow and grief; so speak peace to the winds of trial, as a devout musing upon the subject of the Godhead."

The line which most resonated with me above is when Spurgeon tells us to "be lost in his immensity." Can we stand before the immensity of God Almighty, and retain even a shred of pride? I think not. I believe the single greatest weapon we have in the battle against our own pride and egos is the Word of God. The Apostle Paul writes about the armor of God in Ephesians 6. He writes in verse 17 to take the "sword of the spirit, which is the word of God." It's interesting that Paul uses the Greek word "Rhema" when referring to the "word of God." This word specifically means "spoken word" or "utterance," implying that we weaponize scripture against the devil when we speak it aloud to combat temptation. Consider Jesus prior to His ministry. He is out in the wilderness and Satan comes to tempt him. Satan poses three different temptations to Jesus, and each time, He responds by quoting scripture.

When we immerse ourselves in the Word of God; when we bathe our souls in the study of the Almighty, our awareness of our corrupt nature becomes greatly amplified. We begin to recognize not simply the profane words that we utter, but the profane heart from which they flow. We begin to recognize where a natural thought can lead to a sinful thought, which leads to a sinful action and eventually to the subsequent brokenness we see all over our world today.

James 1:14-15 says:

"But each person is tempted when he is lured and enticed by his own desire. Then desire when it has conceived gives birth to sin, and sin when it is fully grown brings forth death."

But how are we to even begin to recognize these patterns if we ourselves don't know the God who defines what sin is, or more appropriately, what it is not? The word for sin in Ancient Greek "Hamartia" was actually an archery term meaning to "miss the mark." Being created in the image of God, our mark is just that: God's perfection. This is why it is so imperative that we know who God is, otherwise we are flying blind. As we grow in our knowledge of God, and we take the time to bask in His "immensity," there truly remains no basis for our egotistical thoughts. His attributes are relatable, yet simultaneously far beyond our comprehension.

Some of the attributes are the following:

God is **immutable**, or unchanging. God says this of himself in Malachi 3:6

"I am the Lord, I change not…"

This is such a crucial doctrine for us as believers to grasp. The God that burned Sodom & Gomorrah with fire, turned Lot's wife into a pillar of salt, and killed nearly everyone on the planet with a massive flood is the same God that lived humbly amongst us, teaching us gently and lovingly. The same God that was scourged with the utmost brutality and crucified to pay the debt of our sins. He did not change from the Old Testament to the New Testament. The covenant under which we operate with Him has changed be He himself never changes. In theology, we categorize the various attributes of God into two primary divisions. We call this the goodness and severity of God. Both are equal parts of the nature of God and have been for eternity, and will continue to be so, for our God changes not.

God is **self-existent**. No one created God. He depends not on anyone else for his existence or happiness. God is — because He is. This is most plainly evidenced by His name, Yahweh. "I Am." One of my favorite passages from the Gospels is when we see Jesus using this name in reference to himself. God the Son, in the flesh using His name. The name above all names. Let's take a walk for a moment in the Garden of Gethsemane. It's the night of Jesus' betrayal and arrest. Jesus has been praying for what has likely been hours when Judas arrives with the temple guard to arrest Jesus. When Jesus asks the guards "Who are you looking for?" They reply, "Jesus of Nazareth." This is where the special effects come in!

"Jesus said to them, "I am he. Judas, who betrayed him was standing with them. When Jesus said to them, "I am he," they drew back and fell to the ground."

-    *John 18:5-6*

I can't read this passage without seeing this group of temple guards getting knocked clean off their feet in a scene like something out of the Matrix. One has to wonder what went through those guards' heads when that happened? Another detail we miss in translation is the simple fact that the phrase Jesus used was really just "I am." There was no "he." It was just "I am."

Several other attributes of God are His supremacy, sovereignty, faithfulness, grace, patience, mercy, love, power, holiness and wrath. We can see many examples of each of these all throughout scripture, and they are all valuable beyond measure. Our place as believers is to submit to Him, including the full collection of His attributes, as Lord & King.

"Submit yourselves therefore to God. Resist the devil, and he will flee from you. Draw near to God, and he will draw near to you…Humble yourselves before the Lord and he will exalt you."

-    *James 4:7-8; 10*

Chapter 4

Biblical Narcissists

*"Now I, Nebuchadnezzar, praise and extol and honor the King of heaven,
for all his works are right and his ways are just; and those who walk in
pride he is able to humble."*
Daniel 4:37

Nebuchadnezzar

Quite possibly my favorite scriptural example of a prideful man being humbled would be that of the Babylonian Emperor Nebuchadnezzar. Prior to his conquering of the nation of Israel, the Prophet Jeremiah warned the Israelites over and over again that if they did not repent of their idolatry, God would send Nebuchadnezzar to conquer them, and he would lead them out of their land and into captivity. This is precisely what happened in 586 B.C. Shortly after this, Babylon grew to become one of the greatest empires the world has ever seen. Not surprisingly, their emperor Nebuchadnezzar had quite the inflated ego.

After conquering the nation of Israel in 586 B.C. the Jews enter a period of biblical history known as the Babylonian Captivity. You may also see it referred to as the Babylonian Exile, or Exilic period. Many Israelites during this time were sent far away from their homes to Babylon as slaves. However, amid this tumultuous time, we learn of several popular names from the Old Testament. These are Daniel, Shadrach, Meshach, and Abednego. Were it not for the Babylonian Captivity, we wouldn't have some of the incredible stories of the faith such as Daniel and the Lions Den, or Shadrach, Meshach, and Abednego in the fiery furnace, not to mention Daniel's prophetic interpretations of Nebuchadnezzars dreams. These four men were known as "magi" which, unbeknownst to many, is the same word that we translate to "wise men" in the nativity story." So, when the "wise men" or "magi" show up on the scene after Jesus was born, they likely had been reading from the prophet Daniel, and searching for the Messiah, or "anointed one." More than likely, these magi had been reading Daniel chapter 9, which actually gives a tangible timeline starting from the decree to rebuild Jerusalem by Artaxerxes in 457 B.C. to what many scholars believe is the date of the triumphal entry. It quite literally predicts the time of the Messiah's arrival. It really is a fascinating study. And we'd have none of this were it not for our narcissistic friend King Nebuchadnezzar.

The story of Nebuchadnezzars humbling begins in Daniel 2, when Nebuchadnezzar has a dream about a giant statue that terrifies him, rendering him unable to sleep. He summons all of the magi, diviners, enchanters and sorcerers in the palace to come interpret his dream. However, in a manner that only Nebuchadnezzar himself could execute, he refuses to tell his dream to any of them because he doesn't trust them and thinks that they have conspired to tell him lies, which is not entirely wrong. He eventually gets angry and orders that they all be executed. When Arioch, the captain of the king's guard finds Daniel, Daniel has Arioch take him before King Nebuchadnezzar who grants him a short amount of time to pray and seek God on the matter. God reveals to Daniel the precise details of Nebuchadnezzars dream and the interpretation. At this point, Nebuchadnezzar is amazed by the power of Yahweh, the God of Israel, and appoints Daniel as head over all the magi in Babylon, extolling the Lord for His greatness.

In his dream, the Statue is comprised of 5 different sections. The head is made of gold. The chest and arms of silver. It's mid-section and thighs of bronze. It's legs of iron. And the feet were a mix of iron and clay. In the interpretation, Nebuchadnezzar is the golden head. Each other section represents another empire to come after the fall of Babylon. Daniel essentially tells his emperor, King Nebuchadnezzar, that his Kingdom is going to come to an end. One did not simply tell the King something of those sorts. That's just asking to be put to death. However, even Nebuchadnezzar can't deny the fact that God clearly showed Daniel the dream and its interpretation.

Interestingly enough, the very next chapter in Daniel is the Golden Image and the Fiery Furnace. Essentially, Nebuchadnezzar has a massive golden image set up and orders everyone in the Kingdom to worship the golden statue. What we are not told, but many scholars agree on, is what the golden image actually was. Many believe that because of the sequence of events, the golden image was a statue of Nebuchadnezzar himself. Keep in mind, the statue in chapter 2 had him as the golden head, but that meant that his empire would eventually fall to another, which was the Persian Empire represented by the silver arms and chest. So, it wouldn't be a far stretch to imply that the golden statue he erects in chapter 3, this time completely of gold, is of himself, as if to say: "I and my Empire are here to stay." We are in fact, talking about yet another narcissist emperor.

As the story unfolds, Shadrach, Meshach and Abednego refuse to worship the statue and are thrown into the fiery furnace, at which point God rescues them from the fire in quite possibly the "hottest" miracle in the Bible. After this Nebuchadnezzar praises God for how He was able to rescue the three of them out of the fire.

Ole Nebby is such an interesting character in that we see his massively inflated ego get deflated by the mighty works of the Lord, only to go right back to how it was beforehand. However, he seems to reach a point of true repentance and trusting in the Lord at the end of his life.

In Daniel 4, Nebuchadnezzar has yet another dream and he calls Daniel in to interpret it, this time with an entirely different attitude of course. To make a long story short, Nebuchadnezzar essentially ends up losing his mind for a period of time, living out in the field and eating grass like a cow. God restores Nebuchadnezzar's mind and what we see following this is one of the most beautiful, almost cinematic moments of repentance in the entire Bible.

*"But at the end of those days, I, Nebuchadnezzar, lifted up my eyes toward heaven, and my knowledge returned to me, and I blessed the Most High and praised and honored Him who lives forever; For His dominion is an everlasting dominion, And His kingdom endures from generation to generation. "And all the inhabitants of the earth are accounted as nothing, But He does according to His will in the host of heaven and among the inhabitants of earth; And no one can strike against His hand or say to Him, 'What have You done?' At that time my knowledge returned to me. And my majesty and splendor were returned to me for the glory of my kingdom, and my high officials and my nobles began seeking me out; so I was reestablished in my kingdom, and extraordinary greatness was added to me. Now I, Nebuchadnezzar, praise, exalt, and honor the King of heaven, for all His works are true and His ways just, **and He is able to humble those who walk in pride.**"*

-   *Daniel 4:34-37*

This is the last we hear of Nebuchadnezzar aside from Daniel referring back to him after his death, but I tend to believe we may one day meet a very humble Nebuchadnezzar who continues to exalt the name that is above every name! We see in these chapters, God revealing himself to Nebuchadnezzar bit by bit. My hope is that God uses all these passages that we are looking at to reveal himself in greater measure to you and your family.

Peter

The New Testament is encumbered with literature both by, and about, heroes of the early church. We see the life of Christ Himself, the proliferation of the Gospel throughout the Roman Empire. We see the Apostle Paul's radical conversion and subsequent ministry filled with grand tales of persecution, miracles and shipwrecks. There is one such "conversion story" if you will, that stands alone in its uniqueness. That is of Peter the Apostle.

The earliest interaction we see between Jesus and Peter in the New Testament would be in John 1:41-42, in which Peters brother Andrew comes to Peter to tell him "We have found the Messiah!" In these short couple of verses, we find the moment that Jesus renames Simon, the brother of Andrew to Cephas, or Peter; both meaning

"Rock" in their perspective languages of Aramaic & Greek. Keep in mind, as far as we know this is the first encounter that Peter is having with Jesus. I can't help but wonder what went through Peter's head at this moment. Jesus still hasn't called him to be a disciple. They've just met, and Jesus is renaming him? I wonder if Peter was at all agitated by this gesture. And why did Jesus choose to call him "rock?"

Many scholars have argued that this was because of the words that Jesus would later speak in Matthew 16:18

"And I tell you, you are Peter, and on this rock I will build my church, and the gates of hell shall not prevail against it."

The context of this verse definitely seems to support this interpretation, however others have argued that Jesus was referring back to himself as the rock on which He would build His church. This interpretation finds much of its support in Peter's own epistle written decades later in which Peter is quoting various messianic prophecies referring to the Christ as a "Rock," "Stone" and "Cornerstone." (1Peter 2:4-8)

Neither interpretation has major theological ramifications, aside from certain denominations of Christianity "venerating" Peter, primarily due to the former interpretation of this passage. As I read this (don't quote me on this, as this is mainly comedic in nature) I can't help but wonder if Jesus wasn't naming

Peter "rock" because of his stubbornness and pride
which we see very clearly throughout the Gospels.

Take for instance when Jesus foretells Peter's
denial in Matthew 26. We tend to attribute this passage
to Peter specifically, however Jesus tells the disciples
that they will ALL fall away. The initial statement
wasn't to Peter in particular, however, Peter had a
tendency to speak before his mind could catch up. In
fact, Peter is often referred to in modern times as the
"foot in mouth" disciple, due to this unfortunate
predisposition.

*'Peter answered him, "Though they all fall away
because of you, I will never fall away." Jesus said to
him, "Truly, I tell you, this very night, before the rooster
crows, you will deny me three times." Peter said to him,
"Even if I must die with you, I will not deny you!" And
all the disciples said the same.'*

- *Matthew 26:33-35*

So, what happened later that night? Well, after Jesus
was arrested, we see one of the disciples sticking close to
Jesus throughout the night, but it wasn't Peter. It was
John. Now, to Peter's credit, he did go to the courtyard
of the high priest as Jesus was being questioned by the
high priest. Doctor Luke tells us that Peter "followed at a
distance." (Luke 22:54) This is still more than can be
said for the other 9 disciples (not counting Judas for

obvious reasons). John also records that Peter stood warming himself by a charcoal fire. This small detail will find its reprisal several chapter later.

Regarding Peter's denial, Luke gives us a detailed account of Peter's denial of Jesus in Luke 22:54-62, however in verse 61 & 62 you can almost hear the shattering of Peter's pride. As Jesus foretold, Peter denies Jesus three times, and then the rooster crowed:

'And the Lord turned and looked at Peter. And Peter remembered the Lord, how he had said to him, "Before the rooster crows today, you will deny me three times." And he went out and wept bitterly.'

–   Luke 22:61-62

Can you imagine the guilt which Peter must have felt? Here is the Messiah, whom he was followed for several years now, and seen working incredible miracles; the one he claimed to love so much that he would die for. Yet in Jesus' darkest moment, Peter denies even knowing him. One thing to keep in mind is that Luke was not a disciple of Jesus. However, being a doctor and very well educated, Luke did extensive research and took great care to provide a very detailed account of the life of Jesus. In the book of Acts, which is essentially The Gospel According to Luke Volume 2, we see Doctor Luke traveling with Peter & Paul. Much of the details that Luke would've gotten in his research for both the Gospel of Luke and the Acts of the Apostles, would've likely been directly from Peter, whilst also possibly utilizing the Gospel of Mark as a reference.

I picture Luke sitting around a fire with Peter, taking notes as Peter reminisces about his time with Jesus. All at once, Peter gets choked up and a tear begins trickling down his cheek as he tells Doctor Luke the story of how he denied Jesus. I wonder if Luke asked Peter about the details of the crucifixion. And if so, how did Peter manage to get the words out: "I wasn't there."

We don't see Peter at the crucifixion, but only John. Peter remains relatively quiet even after the resurrection until John 21 when Jesus appears again to his disciples who are out fishing.

'Just as day was breaking, Jesus stood on the shore; yet the disciples did not know that it was Jesus. Jesus said to them, "Children, do you have any fish?" They answered him, "No." He said to them, "Cast the net on the right side of the boat, and you will find some." So they cast it, and now they were not able to haul it in, because of the quantity of fish. That disciple whom Jesus loved therefore said to Peter, "It is the Lord!" When Simon Peter heard that it was the Lord, he put on his outer garment, for he was stripped for work, and threw himself into the sea. The other disciples came in the boat, dragging the net full of fish, for they were not far from the land, but about a hundred yards off.'

–   John 21:4-8

Peter's reaction to seeing Jesus on the shore is that of the climax to a drama film. I can almost hear "Chariots of Fire" playing softly in the background as Peter "throws himself into the sea." Had Peter spoken to Jesus yet since the resurrection? We know he'd seen him with the other disciples when Jesus appeared to them all behind lock & key. But had Peter spoken to Him yet? Was he speechless? Was he trying to find a way to explain his actions? We can presuppose all we'd like but the answers will likely allude us until we stand before the Lord in glory.

What we do see, however, is the gracious restoration of Peter and the healing that Jesus offered to his soul. Again, as the Gospels are almost cinematic in nature at times, this is a prime example. Jesus finds Peter in the very place that he called him. Peter has been fishing all night without catching a thing, just as he was the night before Jesus called him to be a disciple. Similarly, Jesus tells them to cast out their nets, just once more. At this moment we see the light switch flip in Peter as he "threw himself" into the sea to get to Jesus.

"When they got out on land, they saw a charcoal fire in place, with fish laid out on it, and bread."

-   *John 21:9*

This detail is of no paramount doctrinal significance, but it shows the tender care our Lord has undertaken to reach our hearts. While scripture refers to burning coals several times, the only other direct mention to someone stoking a charcoal fire throughout the Old & New Testaments is when Peter denies Jesus. I imagine that familiar smell must have brought Peter back to that dark moment when he faltered. Yet, Jesus used this to, in essence, set the table for Peter's restoration.

"When they had finished breakfast, Jesus said to Simon Peter, "Simon, son of John, do you love me more than these?" He said to him, "Yes, Lord; you know that I love you." He said to him, "Feed my lambs." He said to him a second time, "Simon, son of John, do you love me?" He said to him, "Yes, Lord; you know that I love you." He said to him, "Tend my sheep." He said to him the third time, "Simon, son of John, do you love me?" Peter was grieved because he said to him the third time, "Do you love me?" and he said to him, "Lord, you know everything; you know that I love you." Jesus said to him, "Feed my sheep."

-    *John 21:15-17*

As Peter denied Jesus thrice, so Jesus offers restoration to each of these failures as he asks Peter three times "Peter, do you love me?" Verse 17 tells us that Peter was grieved that Jesus had asked him a third time. Do you sense the heaviness of Peter's heart in this passage? Jesus knew that in order to be a truly affective disciple, and minister of the Gospel, Peter needed to be brought low. His pride needed to be dealt with before he could accomplish all that the Lord had for him. Peter himself would later write these famous words:

"Humble yourselves therefore under the mighty hand of God so that at the proper time he may exalt you."
  -    *1Peter 5:6*

The prophet Hosea gives us another glimpse into how the Lord works healing and salvation for his people in one of my personal favorite examples of messianic prophecy in Hosea 6:1-2:

"Come, let us return to the Lord; for he has torn us, that he may heal us; he has struck us down, and he will bind us up. After two days he will revive us; on the third day he will raise us up, that we may live before him."

Mike Donehey of the band Tenth Avenue North lyricized this passage in their song You Do All Things Well:

"You break me to bind me,

You hurt me, Lord, to heal me,

You cut me to touch me,

You died to revive me."

We see here the perfect picture of our Father's loving discipline. As God looks into our diseased and broken hearts, He has compassion on us as He desires "that all should reach repentance." (2Peter 3:9) To often though, our pride blinds us to our sins and our own need of repentance, even as believers. Thankfully though, we serve a God who isn't a neglectful father, but one who goes the extra mile to to be sure we grow into the men and women He has created us to be. Proverbs 3:11-12 says,

"My son, do not despise the Lord's discipline or be weary of his reproof, for the Lord reproves him whom he loves, as a father the son in whom he delights."

How beautiful of a thing it is that the Gospel didn't end at the cross. Nor did it end with the resurrection. The Gospel continues as each day sinners are being adopted and brought into the family of God. These children come in dirty. They smell bad. They use offensive language and do all sorts of other things that we know to be offensive to God. And yet, their sanctification is a continuance of the Lord's work through the Holy Spirit. Thank God, He didn't toss me back out on the streets when I failed to act like His child. Thank God Peter's ministry didn't end when he denied Jesus. On the contrary, our Father gets up close and personal. He restores us. Cleanses us. Disciplines us as we need it, and DISCIPLES us constantly. And all of this is because,

"...God so loved the world that he sent his only Son, that whoever believes in him should not perish but have eternal life."

-   John 3:16

Job

The Book of Job has historically been summarized as a story about a man who had it all and lost it because God allowed Satan to take it away. Yet, he never cursed God. While this is an accurate synopsis of the book, I wish to contend that there is a much greater underlying theme throughout the book that is more foundational in nature.

The story begins in chapter one describing Job's vast wealth. Job owned livestock by the thousands, in a manner that would make the Dutton's envious. In chapter two, Satan approaches God and requests permission to test Job's integrity and righteousness. Satan's argument to God is that Job is only faithful because of how greatly God has blessed him. God allows Satan to destroy Job's health, wealth, and kill his family. It is truly a story that we cannot insert ourselves into while maintaining any measure of realism.

As the narrative progresses, Job's own wife tells him to "curse God and die." She's quite literally advising Job to curse the Lord so that God will strike him dead. A large portion of the book contains an extensive dialogue between Job and his three friends. Job's friends charge

Job with having brought this downfall upon himself because of sin in his life. They continue back & forth from chapters, four to thirty-one. Twenty-seven chapters of discourse in which Job's friends accuse him of unrighteousness, to which Job defends himself. As the chapters progress, we see Job crying out to the Lord only to have his friends continue to accuse him of unrighteousness. Eventually, in chapter 32, a fourth friend of Job, named Elihu, shows up on the scene. When I first did a deep-dive study into the Book of Job, Elihu instantly became one of my favorite Old Testament characters. Elihu is younger than all the others and therefore respectfully maintains his silence for as long as he can bear it. When Elihu does finally respond to Job and his friends, we see an entirely different perspective that reflects the divine outlook on Job's position.

At the outset of chapter thirty-two, Elihu begins to rebuke every party involved in the previous twenty-seven chapters. He verbally steamrolls over Zohar, Bildad, and Eliphaz (Job's three friends). And then he turns his attention to Job as well.

"So these three men ceased to answer Job, because he was righteous in his own eyes. Then Elihu the son of Barachel the Buzite, of the family of Ram, burned with anger. He burned with anger at Job because he justified himself rather than God. He burned with anger also at Job's three friends because they had found no answer, although they had declared Job to be in the wrong."

Here in chapter thirty-three Elihu begins his three-chapter long rebuke of Job as an attorney cross-examining a defendant on trial.

"Answer me if you can; set your words in order before me; take your stand. Behold, I am toward God as you are;" (v. 5-6)

'You say, "I am pure, without transgression; I am clean, and there is no iniquity in me. Behold he finds occasions against me, he counts me as his enemy..."' (v. 9-10)

'Behold, in this you are not right. I will answer you, for God is greater than man. Why do you contend against him saying "he will answer none of man's words?"' (v.12-13)

Job is essentially contending that the Lord does not answer the prayers of men. Elihu continues in chapter thirty-four with a strong charge against Job:

"What man is like Job, who drinks up scoffing like water, who travels in the company of evildoers and walks with wicked men? For he has said, 'It profits a man nothing that he should take delight in God.'" (v. 7-9)

Let's read that again: **"It profits man nothing that he should delight in God."** These are blasphemous words when we consider them in light of verses such as:

"Delight yourself in the Lord, and he will give you the desires of your heart." (Psalm 37:4)

"You make known to me the path of life; in your presence there is fullness of joy; at your right hand are pleasures forevermore." (Psalm 16:11)

Elihu continues:

"If you are righteous, what do you give him? Or what does he receive from your hand?" (Job 35:7)

"Behold, God is exalted in power; who is a teacher like him? Who has prescribed for him his way, or who can say, 'You have done wrong.'" (Job 36:22-23)

Following Elihu's long-winded monologue, we see the Lord show up and answer Job out of the whirlwind. The word used in Hebrew for whirlwind is the same word for a hurricane. So keep in mind this is no whimsical breeze on an afternoon at the park. I grew up in South Florida and lived through quite a few hurricanes. If you walk out in a hurricane when you're near the eye wall, you'll quickly find that you're just a short gust from blowing away. The rain travels quite literally parallel to the ground. These storms uproot trees, tear off roofs, and demolish entire houses. This is the kind of power in which the Lord shows up to speak with Job in chapter thirty-eight:

"Who is this that darkens counsel by words without knowledge? Dress for action like a man; I will question you and you make it known to me." (v. 2-3)

'"Where were you when I laid the foundation of the earth? Tell me, if you have understanding. Who determined its measurements—surely you know! Or who stretched the line upon it? On what were its bases sunk, or who laid its cornerstone, when the morning stars sang together and all the sons of God shouted for joy? "Or who shut in the sea with doors when it burst out from the womb, when I made clouds its garment and thick darkness its swaddling band, and prescribed limits for it and set bars and doors, and said, 'Thus far shall you come, and no farther, and here shall your proud waves be stayed'? (v. 4-11)

"Have you comprehended the expanse of the earth? Declare, if you know all this." (V.18)

"Do you know the ordinances of the heavens? Can you establish their rule on the earth? (V. 33)

Then God really challenges Job:

"Shall a faultfinder contend with the Almighty? He who argues with God, let him answer it." (Job 40:2)

At this point we see a very fearful and humble Job answer in a manner in which you can nearly hear the cracking in his voice:

*"Behold, I am of small account; what shall I answer
you? I lay my hand on my mouth. I have spoken once,
and I will not answer twice, but I will proceed no
further." (Job 40: 4-5)*

At this point, Job seems to be regretting his previous
decision to justify himself to God, who has essentially
said to Job, "You want to fight? Let's go. Man up!" But
Job is beginning to turn around. He's beginning to make
that 180 degree turn of repentance. However, God
doesn't let up quite yet.

*"Dress for action like a man; I will question you and you
make it known to me. Will you even put me in the wrong?
Will you condemn me that you may be in the right? Have
you an arm like God, and can you thunder with a voice
like his?" (Job 40:7-9)*

*"Look on everyone who is proud and bring him low…"
(Job 40:12)*

The final chapter of Job, we see Job's confession and
repentance, The Lord rebuking Job's three friends, and
God restoring Job's fortunes.

*'Then Job answered the Lord and said: "I know that you
can do all things, and that no purpose of yours can be
thwarted. 'Who is this that hides counsel without
knowledge?' Therefore I have uttered what I did not
understand, things too wonderful for me, which I did not
know. 'Hear, and I will speak; I will question you, and
you make it known to me.' I had heard of you by the*

hearing of the ear, but now my eye sees you; therefore I despise myself, and repent in dust and ashes." ' (Job 42:1-6)

As first world humans living in the twenty-first century, with all of our personal liberties which we have great reason to be thankful for, we often take a humanistic perspective on stories like these. We tend to question God and his justice, much like Job did. And if we are honest with ourselves, I'm certain that none of us would have faired as well as Job. And still, the Lord found cause to rebuke Job in such a way as we just looked at.

The Apostle Paul, faced with answering the Romans on the doctrine of election gave a similar response. I don't wish to argue the doctrine of election in this book, however what I do feel compelled to uphold is the sovereignty and supremacy of God. This is, I believe, the theme of most crucial imperativeness in Romans 9.

'What shall we say then? Is there injustice on God's part? By no means! For he says to Moses, "I will have mercy on whom I have mercy, and I will have compassion on whom I have compassion." So then it depends not on human will or exertion, but on God, who has mercy. For the Scripture says to Pharaoh, "For this very purpose I have raised you up, that I might show my power in you, and that my name might be proclaimed in all the earth." So then he has mercy on whomever he wills, and he hardens whomever he wills. You will say to

*me then, "Why does he still find fault? For who can
resist his will?" But who are you, O man, to answer
back to God? Will what is molded say to its molder,
"Why have you made me like this?"'*

-      *Romans 9:14-20*

As previously stated, I'm not including this text to argue
for or against the doctrine of election. I don't wish to
stoke the fire between my Calvinist and Arminian
brothers. The fire I wish to fan into flame is that of a
passion for God's sovereignty and supremacy. When
Paul says, "Who are you, oh man, to answer back to
God?" in verse 20 that should smash our pride like a
sledgehammer. Paul is saying "Who do you think you
are?" The Lord was asking Job, "Who do you think you
are?" It is of utmost importance that we allow these
passages to reorient our hearts on who is God and who is
not. We must not allow our ever-so-cherished liberties to
give us a false sense of self-importance in the Kingdom
of God. God is God and we are not. We must know our
place, and thankfully because of what our Lord and
savior has accomplished for us, our place is as children
of God almighty. Sons and daughters of the King of
glory.

Belshazzar

In his iconic song released in 1978, Cats in The
Cradle, Harry Chapin followed the lives of a father and
son, beginning when the son was born in verse one. As is
unfortunately more common than not, the father, who
clearly loved his son, kept so busy throughout the boy's
childhood that he missed seeing his son learn to walk.
He told his son that he had too much on his plate to teach
him to throw a ball. When the boy comes home from
college, the tides begin to turn as the boy doesn't care to
take the time to spend with his dad. In the final verse, the
father calls up his son who has moved away and asks to
get together. The son tells him he'd love to but is so busy
with work and his kids that he can't. That's when reality
hits the father, and he realizes that his son has become
him.

As children mirror and imitate the actions they
witness growing up, so Belshazzar witnessed the pride
ands arrogance of his father… Nebuchadnezzar. Before
we go too far into this story, it's important that we do
our due diligence in understanding the relational aspect
here. Belshazzar is not actually Nebuchadnezzar's son.
There is no firm consensus on the exact relationship
between the two, however, secular history tells us that
Belshazzar's father was the Babylonian King Nabonidus,
who succeeded the throne shortly after the death of
Nebuchadnezzar. The two primary trains of thought
regarding the relationship between Nebuchadnezzar and
Belshazzar, and the mention of their paternal relationship
in Daniel chapter five, are as follows:

First, some scholars believe that the application of
the word "father" to Nebuchadnezzar is simply referring
to succession of the throne. Essentially, this would be
like someone referring to the current President of the
United States as the "son" of George Washington,
Abraham Lincoln, or Dwight D. Eisenhower. This
practice was not entirely uncommon in the ancient
middle east which provides added validity to this
position.

The second option that many biblical scholars hold to
is that Belshazzar was Nebuchadnezzar's grandson.
Since we know that Belshazzar's father was Nabonidus,
that rules out Nebuchadnezzar. However, it is possible
that Belshazzar's mother was one of the daughters of
Nebuchadnezzar, who married Nabonidus. This
supposition is not currently verifiable, however the
context of Daniel 5 gives us as students of the Bible,
good reason to believe that Belshazzar was likely
Nebuchadnezzar's grandson. In Daniel 5,
Nebuchadnezzar is referred to as Belshazzar's father on
seven separate occasions. But did we not just agree that
Belshazzar's father was actually Nabonidus? That's
where ancient Hebrew often throws us little curve balls
here and there. The word for father "ab" is the same
word for grandfather, great-grandfather, great-great-
grandfather and so on. More than likely, Daniel is
speaking to Belshazzar about his grandfather.

While this debate may seem trivial, we as believers
are told to be ready at all times to defend our hope in the
Gospel. The apostle Peter tells us in 1 Peter 3:15

"...but in your hearts honor Christ the Lord as holy, always being prepared to make a defense to anyone who asks you for a reason for the hope that is in you; yet do it with gentleness and respect."

Secular critics have for centuries attempted to disprove the book of Daniel, to no avail, using poor logical fallacies, often to be superseded by archaeological findings. This relationship between Nebuchadnezzar and Belshazzar is no exception.

Quite possibly the most recognizable aspect of Daniel 5 and the story of Belshazzar is the handwriting on the wall. As Belshazzar is throwing a party, he ordered the "golden vessels" that had been taken out of the temple in Jerusalem when Nebuchadnezzar besieged the temple in 586 B.C. to be brought in that he, his lords, his wives and his concubines might drink from them. As they drank from them, they also praised the gods of gold, silver, iron, wood, and stone. Immediately a human hand appears, hovering in mid-air, writing on the plaster something that no one can read. Verse six tells us that Belshazzars color changed, his limbs gave way, and his knees knocked together. When he finally summons Daniel, per the recommendation of the Queen, Daniel comes in and interprets the writing on the wall. There is one aspect of this story that is quite comical in nature and makes me laugh every time I read this passage. Belshazzar offers whoever can interpret the writing on the wall to wear robes of purple, a gold chain to be around their neck, and to be made third in all of the

Kingdom of Babylon. Daniel's apathy towards this regal offer is fantastically hilarious:

"Let your gifts be for yourself and give your rewards to another. Nevertheless, I will read the writing to the king and make known its interpretation." (Daniel 5:17)

At this point, Daniel is advanced in years and served Nebuchadnezzar throughout nearly his entire reign as head of the King's Magi. God has given him miraculous revelations of dreams and their interpretations. He's seen his three friends thrown into a furnace and come out without a hair on their heads singed. Daniel is unfazed by Belshazzar's generous offer, and apparently any consequence he might procure as a result of what appears at first glance to be a rather irreverent response to the King.

Daniel then begins his address to King Belshazzar by speaking of the greatness of Nebuchadnezzar, and how God humbled him as he says in verse 20:

"But when his heart was lifted up and his spirit was hardened so that he dealt proudly, he was brought down from his kingly throne, and his glory was taken from him."

At this point, Daniel turns the focus on Belshazzar:

"And you his son, Belshazzar have not humbled your heart, though you knew all this, but you have lifted

yourself up against the Lord of heaven." (Daniel 5:22-23)

"...but the God in whose hand is your breath, and whose are all your ways you have not honored." (Daniel 5:23)

It is at this point that Daniel begins to interpret the "writing on the wall." In the 2001 film, A Knights Tale, our antagonist Count Adhemar (played by Rufus Sewell), says to the central character William Thatcher (played by Heath Ledger) during a jousting match:

"You have been weighed; you have been measured; and you have been found wanting."

This famous line is actually a paraphrase from Daniel 5:27 when Daniel interprets the writing on the wall for Belshazzar.

"MENE, God has numbered the days of your kingdom and brought it to an end; TEKEL, you have been weighed in the balances and found wanting; PERES, your Kingdom is divided and given to the Medes and Persians." (Daniel 5:26-28)

Remember when we saw how Daniel declined Belshazzar's grand offer of riches and status in a rather contemptuous manner? Apparently, Belshazzar had already forgotten about this interchange because as soon as Daniel finishes interpreting the writing on the wall, in which he tells Belshazzar that his kingdom has come to an end (which you simply didn't say to a king unless you had a death-wish), verse 29 tells us:

"Then Belshazzar gave the command, and Daniel was clothed with purple, a chain of gold was put around his neck and a proclamation was made about him, that he should be the third ruler in the kingdom."

I can't help but wonder if Daniel was thinking to himself "Please stop. You're going to get me killed by the new King." And what proceeds after these verses in secular history is positively fascinating! Cyrus of Persia had determined in his mind to conquer Babylon, which would have been nearly impossible by conventional warfare. So, Cyrus devised a plan utilizing the design of the city of Babylon against itself. The city's outer wall lined the Euphrates River with a series of gates along the wall. The Euphrates, however, was a very large and powerful river that was only passable by boat, making an invasion along the river impossible. Cyrus however, found a way to do the impossible. He dug a series of canals along the Euphrates to empty it into a large reservoir, therein lowering the river to about knee deep, allowing his soldiers to cross the river on foot, and sneak under the gates of the outer wall and into the city under the cover of darkness.

The most riveting part of these two accounts is how precisely they line up. Daniel 5:30 says "That very night Belshazzar the Chaldean King was killed, and Darius the Mede received the kingdom…" If you're confused as to why Darius the Mede receives the

Kingdom when Cyrus of Persia devised this whole takeover scheme, they are often referred to in conjunction as the Medo-Persian Empire. As a matter of fact, Darius the Mede is the king in power who has Daniel thrown in the lions' den, and after him, we see Cyrus reigning when Ezra and a host of Israelites are sent to rebuild the Temple in Jerusalem.

What I find so captivating about this story is how God didn't simply strike Belshazzar dead for his pride and arrogance. Rather, God raised up his enemy Cyrus, and had a plan in motion long before its execution. This follows right along with the plan for salvation that God had in place before the foundations of the world. Long before Adam and Eve ate of the fruit of the tree. There are no Plan B's with God, yet He has offered each of us a second chance through His own blood. When we hold a right view of this Gospel, we'll find that we haven't a leg to stand on in the presence of God Almighty. How on earth can we continue, having hearts full of pride, when the infinite God humbled himself; was born into the world, covered in amniotic fluid like the rest of us; lived a life of rejection and ridicule; and was tortured and hung (likely naked) on a cross for OUR sins. This, my friends, is why ego, pride and arrogance have no place in a follower of Christ. We need to "put to death what is earthly in us," as the Apostle Paul said in Colossians 3:5. To echo once more the puritan John Owen, we need to be killing sin before it kills us, and that begins with renewing out minds (Romans 12:2) in the Word of God and the Gospel of Jesus Christ.

"For the one who sows to his own flesh will from the flesh reap corruption, but the one who sows to the Spirit will from the Spirit reap eternal life."
-   Galatians 6:8

Chapter 5

Biblical Humility

"When pride comes, then comes disgrace, but with the humble is wisdom."
Proverbs 11:2

King David

While preparing and studying for this book, I found myself at a bit of a crossroads in character organization. We've looked at a variety of biblical figures from both the Old and New Testaments in the previous chapter who depict for us the effects of unrepentant pride. Conversely, I want to look at various characters who embody the very idea of biblical humility. Herein lies the dilemma I faced. What about King David? My pastor mentioned him as an example of pride. And there is certainly one glaring example of this in 2 Samuel 11& 12 when David see's Bathsheba bathing on her rooftop, commits adultery with her, and then tries to cover up the whole ordeal by conspiring to have her husband killed in battle. Nothing major… However, we also see a true and sincere repentance in David just after this.

I just finished teaching the last two weeks at different churches on hearing God's voice, and the primary character that we looked at for their genuine passion for the Lord was King David. With that stated, I don't believe pride and genuineness can coexist without serious internal resistance, for the prideful man cares about appearance and reputation over authenticity of the heart; and the man with a genuine heart will treasure this authenticity and integrity over the opinions of others. This is quite apparent of David in 2 Samuel chapter 6 when David dances before the Lord in nothing but a linen ephod. If you're not familiar with the term "linen ephod," it refers to what men wore as underwear back in biblical times. Essentially, David was dancing through the streets of Jerusalem in nothing but a loin cloth. He was worshiping in his "tighty whiteys."

Some scholars have argued that this passage doesn't say that David danced in his underwear due in part to the fact that an ephod was also part of the priestly wardrobe, however this is where a class on hermeneutics, or the study of reading and interpreting scripture, could benefit each of us a great deal. Any time we're reading a passage of scripture, we always need to think about the context.

Who: Who is speaking to who in this passage?

What: What are they talking about? What happens just before and after this passage?

When: What period of time is this and how should I therefore read this passage?

Where: Where is this taking place and how does that effect the context?

Why: Why is God's Word telling me this, and what is the point He is trying to drive home?

When we apply these principles to our study of God's Word, we will quickly begin to understand it in a much deeper way; I believe, the way in which God intended for us to understand them.

Therefore, as we utilize these tools in 2 Samuel 6, we find that just after verse 14 which reads: "And David danced before the Lord with all his might. And David was wearing a linen ephod…" we also see in verse 20 how upset David's wife Michal was with his behavior.

"How the King of Israel honored himself today, uncovering himself today before the eyes of his servants' female servants, as one of the vulgar fellows shamelessly uncovers himself!"

Clearly, Michal was not referring to a priestly head covering, nor was she a fan of David's behavior. In her defense, i'm certain that my wife would feel the same way if this were me! After this, David really lit into his wife, bringing up both her father, and the female servants that she spoke of. Gentleman, sometimes I think the Lord slips in little details into scripture as lessons. This was **clearly** a lesson on what **not** to say to your wife in an argument! As a matter of fact, verse 23 tells us, "And Michal the daughter of Saul had no child to the day of her death."

David apparently slept on the couch for the remainder of his reign as king! I was recently preaching at a senior adult revival at our church and went through this passage when one of the older ladies in the congregation said to me after the service "Maybe that's why David was looking at Bathsheba!" Needless to say, I laughed my socks off.

In verse 22 David says to Michal, *"I will become even more undignified than this, and I will be humiliated in my own eyes."*

David isn't concerned with what others are thinking of him. David is only concerned with praising and glorifying the Lord; inasmuch that he is willing to humiliate himself, even as king, before his own servants. This attitude is quite the opposite of the pompous pride that we see in other kings and emperors throughout history.

Consider for a moment the story of Queen Esther. When she is tasked by the Lord through her cousin Mordecai to intercede to King Xerxes (Ahasuerus) on behalf of her people, she is painfully aware of one fearful fact: it was a crime punishable by death for anyone to appear before the King uninvited.

These Persian Kings thought so highly of themselves that they wouldn't hesitate to execute someone just for *attempting* to speak to them.

In 2Samuel 6:21, David reminds his wife Michal, the daughter of the late King Saul, that it was the Lord who chose him over her father to be King over Israel. If we jump back to 1 Samuel 13:14 we will find that the prophet Samuel was speaking to Saul about this very thing:

"But now your kingdom shall not continue. The Lord has sought out a man after his own heart, and the Lord has commanded him to be prince over his people…"

This verse really sealed the deal for me on choosing to focus on David's humility over his pride. I believe David likely struggled with pride about as much as any man with his reputation and power would. Yet, each time that David leads his armies to victory, we don't see him taking credit for being a great warrior and king. Rather, we see him glorifying God for giving them the victory, and I believe that's precisely why God calls David a man after his own heart. No one else in the Bible is given this "title." Yet the Lord saw something special in the heart of His servant David that reflected his image in a way in which we were all originally intended to do so.

I wonder what stage of life King David was in when he wrote Psalm 138. Where was he at? Had he recently defeated Goliath as a young lad after stepping forward in faith to be used by the Lord to deliver the Israelites? Was he hiding from his son Absalom who had come to usurp his throne? Could it be that he was watching his young son Solomon as he played about in his throne room and reminiscing about how the Lord had taken a dark moment in David's life, and redeemed it through his new son who would one day become King and construct the Temple of the Lord? Remember that the Gospel of Matthew traces Jesus' lineage back for us through Solomon, the son of David & Bathsheba, lest we forget that the Lord can redeem any circumstance for His own good and glory!

If you can't tell by now, I'm very much so a fan of the Old Testament. While we garner the majority of our doctrine in regard to the Gospel from the New Testament, The Old Testament reveals to us the attributes of God in a way that is entirely proprietary. We need always to remember that God did not change between the Old and New Testaments. I stated this earlier in chapter 3 and will do so again because I believe the immutability of God is a doctrine that desperately needs to be driven home in the hearts of contemporary believers. If our God is truly perfect in every way, then there is no need for Him to grow or change. In fact, The Lord Himself tells us in Malachi 3:6 "For I the Lord do not change…"

Many Christians in our modern world have grasped onto the false idea that once upon a time, we had an "angry God" in the Old Testament, but Jesus came to set the record straight and now we have a "loving God" in the New Testament. This perception is entirely false. The same God who turned Lot's wife into a pillar of salt, flooded the earth, killing everyone but Noah's family, and rained fire on Sodom & Gommorah is the same God who was born to a virgin in a humble feeding trough, lived a perfect, sinless life, died a torturous death, and three days later rose again so that "whosoever believes in him should not perish but have everlasting life." (Jn. 3:16) This same God will return one day to make war on the devil, his kingdom, and execute judgement on sin. The apparent dichotomy in these attributes and works of God are simply two sides of the same coin.

While the covenant under which we operate with Him has changed, He has not. It's for this very reason that I believe we as christians should be diving into the Old Testament just as much as the New Testament. God's word reveals so much about His character, and we see this so clearly in King David.

If we look back to the story of David and Bathsheba again, we will find in 2 Samuel 12:15 that the Lord afflicts the newborn child of David & Bathsheba so that the child becomes sick. To make a long story short,

David fasted and prayed for seven days for his child, and at the end of the seven days, the child dies. At this point, I don't think I could in good conscience give an assessment as to how I would handle this if I were in David's position. However, I'm pretty certain that it wouldn't be quite what David did.

"Then David arose from the earth and washed and anointed himself and changed his clothes. And he went into the house of the Lord and worshipped."

- *2 Samuel 12:20*

When David sees that God's answer to his seven days of prayer and fasting was simply put, "no…" his first response isn't to get angry and curse God. It isn't to go and wail and mourn with those close to him. Both of these would be, at least from a humanistic perspective, reasonable responses to such a tragic loss of a child, not withstanding the circumstances. He didn't even go eat immediately after seven days of fasting. On the contrary, David chooses to clean himself up so that he is able to enter the house of the Lord, and immediately goes and worships God.

How would you respond in this same situation? I'm quite certain that I would not display the same spiritual integrity of David in that moment. Yet, when we step back for a moment of introspection and prayer, we can clearly see where our hearts don't line up with God's heart and ask Him to sanctify us; to be men and women after his own heart as David was.

David further displays his fire for God's glory above his own in his burning passion to build a house for the Lord. We can find this story in 1 Chronicles 17.

'Now when David lived in his house, David said to Nathan the prophet, "Behold, I dwell in a house of cedar, but the ark of the covenant of the Lord is under a tent." And Nathan said to David, "Do all that is in your heart, for God is with you." But that same night the word of the Lord came to Nathan, "Go and tell my servant David, 'Thus says the Lord: It is not you who will build me a house to dwell in. For I have not lived in a house since the day I brought up Israel to this day, but I have gone from tent to tent and from dwelling to dwelling. In all places where I have moved with all Israel, did I speak a word with any of the judges of Israel, whom I commanded to shepherd my people, saying, "Why have you not built me a house of cedar?" ' Now, therefore, thus shall you say to my servant David, 'Thus says the Lord of hosts, I took you from the pasture, from following the sheep, to be prince over my people Israel, and I have been with you wherever you have gone and have cut off all your enemies from before you. And I will make for you a name, like the name of the great ones of the earth. And I will appoint a place for my people Israel and will plant them, that they may dwell in their own place and be disturbed no more. And violent men shall waste them no more, as formerly, from the time that I appointed judges over my people Israel. And I will subdue all your enemies. Moreover, I declare to you that the Lord will build you a house. When your days are fulfilled to walk with your fathers, I will raise up your

offspring after you, one of your own sons, and I will establish his kingdom. He shall build a house for me, and I will establish his throne forever. I will be to him a father, and he shall be to me a son. I will not take my steadfast love from him, as I took it from him who was before you, but I will confirm him in my house and in my kingdom forever, and his throne shall be established forever."

  – *1 Chronicles 17:1-14*

   This same story can also be found in 2 Samuel 7. I think we can all agree that David's heart was in the right place in regard to building the Lord a house. Yet God essentially tells David "No. You can't build me a house."

   1 Chronicles 22:8 tells us that God's reason for denying this privilege to David is because he had been a man of war and shed much blood. If you ever read through the historical books of the Old Testament, you're certain to find that David did in fact kill a lot of people. The Lord only makes a particular point about this when it comes to Uriah the husband of Bathsheba, and building the Temple. Otherwise, God seems to be understanding of David's bloodshed as he was King of Judah and Israel, tasked with protecting the Kingdom of God.

How do you think you would respond to God's answer? I believe the prideful man would retort with something along the lines of: "Fine, you don't want my help? I don't need you either." But how does David respond? He is overjoyed by the goodness of God towards him and the promise of God to his son.

"Then King David went in and sat before the Lord and said, "Who am I, O Lord God, and what is my house, that you have brought me thus far? And this was a small thing in your eyes, O God. You have also spoken of your servant's house for a great while to come, and have shown me future generations, O Lord God! And what more can David say to you for honoring your servant? For you know your servant. For your servant's sake, O Lord, and according to your own heart, you have done all this greatness, in making known all these great things. There is none like you, O Lord, and there is no God besides you, according to all that we have heard with our ears."

    —   1 Chronicles 17:16-20

David's attitude is clearly expressed in his words:

"Who am I?"

"...your servant..."

"There is none like you"

The very next chapter chronicles the stories of David's conquests as King. As the Israelites took the spoils of war from their enemies, David makes a point of dedicating them to the Lord. He sets aside the spoils of war — gold, silver, and bronze — for the future Temple. David made every possible preparation for the construction of the Temple *that he would never see*. He drafted the plans. Had the stones cut in advance. He imported timbers and stored up precious metals in abundance.

'So I have provided for the house of my God, so far as I was able, the gold for the things of gold, the silver for the things of silver, and the bronze for the things of bronze, the iron for the things of iron, and wood for the things of wood, besides great quantities of onyx and stones for setting, antimony, colored stones, all sorts of precious stones and marble. Moreover, in addition to all that I have provided for the holy house, I have a treasure of my own of gold and silver, and because of my devotion to the house of my God I give it to the house of my God: 3,000 talents of gold, of the gold of Ophir, and 7,000 talents of refined silver, for overlaying the walls of the house, and for all the work to be done by craftsmen, gold for the things of gold and silver for the things of silver. Who then will offer willingly, consecrating himself today to the Lord?"'

—   1 Chronicles 29:2-5

We see in this passage that in addition to all his preparations as King, and the items he dedicated to the Lord throughout his reign, King David makes another offering for the construction of the Temple at the end of his life and asks who will join him in offering to the Lord. Sometimes the magnitude of the details can be lost on us in these stories due to the use of ancient units of measurement. So as a point of reference, King David's personal offering in this passage equates to around $30,000,000,000. That's certainly the largest love offering I've ever heard of! This ends up being about 30-40% of the total offering given by all the tribes of Israel towards to construction of the Temple. Yet David doesn't take credit for being the highest donor.

"But who am I, and what is my people, that we should be able thus to offer willingly? For all things come from you, and of your own have we given you."

>   –   *1 Chronicles 29:14*

If only every Christian had a heart like Davids!

Mary

One particular character which scripture doesn't give any excess of attention to would be Mary, the mother of Jesus. Some churches & denominations have spoken of and taught in regard to her more than we see her mentioned in the Bible. This notwithstanding, Mary was indeed a very special young woman who exuded humility and submission to the Lord.

Let's begin with a bit of historical context. Mary was betrothed to a man we all know by the name of Joseph. She was more than likely only 13-14 years old at the time the Holy Spirit conceived the Son of God within her. This may seem at first glance like the pilot episode to a reality tv show from the early 2000's, however marrying young was quite commonplace in the first century Middle East. What was not commonplace, however, was the fact that she was a virgin. The ambiguous nature of her pregnancy was not lost on contemporary Nazarene society either.

There were times during Jesus' ministry in which the Pharisees & Sadducees took shots at Jesus regarding his mothers "virgin conception." One such example is found in John chapter eight. Jesus and the Pharisees are engaging in a bit of "verbal jousting," as was their common practice. The Pharisees are upset by the things that Jesus is teaching, and they attempt to justify themselves as children of Abraham. Eventually, as they really have no other reasonable argument to pose, they take a subtle shot at Jesus via Mary.

'They said to him, "We were not born of sexual immorality. We have one Father—even God."'

— John 8:41

This is an easy verse to glance over and most Christians do, however, when we try to place ourselves there at this conversation, it quickly becomes apparent that the intent of the Pharisees language was to get under Jesus' skin. Their attempt was certainly successful in angering Him as His response was quite impassioned.

"You are of your father the devil, and your will is to do your father's desires. He was a murderer from the beginning, and does not stand in the truth, because there is no truth in him. When he lies, he speaks out of his own character, for he is a liar and the father of lies. But because I tell the truth, you do not believe me. Which one of you convicts me of sin? If I tell the truth, why do you not believe me? Whoever is of God hears the words of God. The reason why you do not hear them is that you are not of God."

–   John 8:44-47

To paraphrase Jesus' first statement here:

"You are sons of the devil, and your will is to do his (the devil) desires."

In other words: Don't mess with Jesus' mama.

Returning our focus to Mary, lets look for a moment at where we first see her. Our good friend Dr. Luke gives us the most detailed account of the nativity story. In chapter one, the angel Gabriel appears to Mary with a message of the utmost importance!

*"And he came to her and said, "Greetings, O favored
one, the Lord is with you!" But she was greatly troubled
at the saying, and tried to discern what sort of greeting
this might be. And the angel said to her, "Do not be
afraid, Mary, for you have found favor with God. And
behold, you will conceive in your womb and bear a son,
and you shall call his name Jesus. He will be great and
will be called the Son of the Most High. And the Lord
God will give to him the throne of his father David, and
he will reign over the house of Jacob forever, and of his
kingdom there will be no end." And Mary said to the
angel, "How will this be, since I am a virgin?" And the
angel answered her, "The Holy Spirit will come upon
you, and the power of the Most High will overshadow
you; therefore, the child to be born will be called holy—
the Son of God. And behold, your relative Elizabeth in
her old age has also conceived a son, and this is the
sixth month with her who was called barren. For nothing
will be impossible with God." And Mary said, "Behold, I
am the servant of the Lord; let it be to me according to
your word." And the angel departed from her."*

    –   Luke 1:28-38

Right away, Gabriel calls Mary "O favored
one…" This isn't the only time in scripture we see the
Lord showing His favor toward a particular individual,
however, it is the only time that I have been able to find
in which the Lord sends an angel to announce the Lord's
favor on a specific person. Moreover, it appears that
Gabriel may even be a bit excited himself to meet the

girl that is going to carry God the Son in her womb and even raise him!

Imagine with me for just a moment, the Lord announcing His plan to Michael and Gabriel. The idea of God Almighty being born to a 13-year-old girl from Nazareth in a feeding trough had to have left them speechless.

"Gabriel, there is a girl from this tiny town called Nazareth that I love dearly. She has my favor and is truly special."

I realize I'm reading into the passage a bit here. Yet, if it were myself in Gabriel's shoes, I would be incredibly excited my entire way to Nazareth to meet the girl that was going to mother the eternal God!

Notice next how Gabriel follows up his opening statement with the one thing that angels seemingly have to reiterate every time they appear to someone in scripture…

"Fear not."

"Do not be afraid."

Apparently, God's angels are quite terrifying because most of the time, grown men would fall on their faces in front of them. Keep in mind they are depicted in "hosts' or "armies" throughout the Old Testament, and again in the Book of Revelation.

In Numbers 22 when the Lord uses Balaam's donkey to speak to him, and then opens his eyes to see the Angel of the Lord, Balaam fell flat on his face in terror. Whatever these creatures look like, I'm most certain it is not effeminate, beardless men with long flowing hair, or floating chubby babies. Unfortunately, pagan mythology began to creep into the church very early on. Particularly after Emperor Constantine issued the Edict of Milan in 313 A.D.

10 years later, Christianity would become the official religion of the Roman Empire. Many holidays we now celebrate actually find their origins in pagan mythology. All of this to say, at times we should step back from our preconceived ideas of biblical subjects such as angels, and heaven, to see what scripture really says about them. I have found that every single time, the Bible's version is far better!

So Gabriel appears to Mary, who is likely terrified. He tells her not to fear not, and delivers to her the gospel message, and her role in it. Next, we have Mary's response. Keep in mind that she is likely only 13-14 years old.

"Behold, I am the servant of the Lord; let it be to me according to your word."

— Luke 1:38

Mary's life would be forever changed after this encounter. Her betrothed, Joseph, would settle to divorce her until God intervened. She would have to birth her first child without her mother or sisters, in a town that was foreign to her. And in a barn, nonetheless.

She would be forced to travel to Egypt for several years to protect her baby from Herod. And she likely heard the words "adulteress" and "whore" spoken quietly as she walked by neighbors in the marketplace. Later on, she would even have to watch this baby, now her grown son, be tortured and killed before her own eyes.

"Behold, I am the servant of the Lord; let it be to me according to your word." (Luke 1:38)

As a man, I often find myself wanting to be like David, or Paul, or Peter. Perhaps though, we all ought to strive to be more like Mary.

Joseph

Most of us, if we grew up in church for any length of time, have heard the tale of Joseph from Genesis 37-47. One of the lengthier stories in Genesis, Joseph's is one of love, family, betrayal, and a host of other obstacles that placed one man in exactly the position that God had predestined for him. Joseph was (and by no means secretly) the favorite son of Jacob.

Born to Rebekah in her old age, Jacob had long desired to father a child with his first wife. This had proven to be an endeavor that yielded no fruit in their youth until at about 91 years old, Jacob finally held baby Joseph in his arms. I'm sure at first this was a joyful occasion for the older sons of Jacob, until the years of favoritism gave rise to a heap of jealousy and covetousness in their hearts. Honestly, I can't entirely blame them for their ill sentiments toward their youngest brother. How they handled that is another thing, but they likely had more than sufficient reason to *want* to do away with him.

Joseph's relationship with his brothers really comes to a head in Genesis 37. First and foremost, Joseph was out pasturing the flocks when upon his return, he brought a bad report to his father regarding his brothers. The Bible even tells us in verse three that Jacob/Israel loved Joseph more than any of his brothers.

One example of this preferential treatment comes directly after the aforementioned statement when Jacob makes the amazing technicolor dream coat, as Andrew Lloyd Webber called it, for young Joseph. Now, we've all heard of Joseph and his "coat of many colors," but this translation comes from the Septuagint, which was a Greek translation of the Torah used for centuries by Jews and non-Jews alike to study the Old Testament in the contemporary vernacular. An alternative translation to this phrase, and likely the more accurate as well, is that Jacob made Joseph a robe with long sleeves. I realize this isn't as exciting as a rainbow robe, but the "long-sleeves" translation fits the context and setting more appropriately than the technicolor dream coat interpretation.

The significance of the long sleeves is actually quite simple. Jacob and his family were nomadic herdsmen. They were essentially ancient middle eastern cowboys, if you will. I used to milk cows at small dairy down the road from my house in South Florida. Once the cows were in their stanchions, every subsequent step was quite particular, though very simple. However, before wiping down the utters or setting up the pump, I always did one simple thing first. I rolled up my sleeves! Lots of things have changed in our world since the time of Jacob (almost 4,000 years ago) and his family. Some things, however, will always be the same. The men out working with their hands each day typically wore short sleeves, or no sleeves at all. Wearing a robe with long sleeves was like having the white-collared architect show up on a construction site. It symbolized authority. It showed that Jacob had given Joseph a special position amongst his brothers, even as the youngest. Verse four tells us that Joseph's brothers hated him for this.

As if these last two items weren't grounds enough for the older eleven brothers to deplore Joseph, this final one really adds insult to injury. Joseph has a dream that he and his brothers are binding wheat sheaves. Suddenly, Joseph's wheat sheave stands upright and all of his brother's sheaves bow to his. Do you think its possible that Joseph might have had a bit of an inflated ego as a result of the persistent nepotism from his father and this newfound gift of his special dreams? The latter part of this story confirms that God did indeed have a purpose in all the chaos that was about to unfold in Joseph's life. I tend to think that the journey was God's way of preparing Josephs heart for the esteemed role he was to play later in his life.

After having their fill of of young Joseph's shenanigans, his older brothers determined to get rid of him one way or another. His brother Judah decides it would be best to sell him as a slave to the Ishmaelites for a grand sum of 20 pieces of silver. Sounds terrible, right? It ought to also sound a bit familiar. Our savior was betrayed by one of his 12 disciples for 30 pieces of silver. And its no mistake that his name was Judas. Judas was simply the "greekified" version of the Hebrew name Judah. Much like Christ, Joseph would suffer greatly to ultimately save a great multitude of people.

Always remember: The Gospel is all over the Old Testament! The theological term for this is "Typology." There are various characters throughout the Old Testament whose stories share striking similarities to that of Christ Jesus. This is because they were a "type" of the one to come.

At this point, Joseph is sold to a prominent Egyptian man named Potiphar, the captain of Pharaoh's guard. Genesis 39 tells us that the Lord caused Joseph to succeed in all that he did and gave him favor in the sight of his master. I've certainly had times in my own life where I could sense that the Lord was giving me great favor in the work of my hands. It was easy to see that it was all because of His hand of favor. All I was doing at the time was being willing and trying to stay humble. On the other hand, I've had times where my heart wasn't focused on doing His work, and I began to take credit for the success that the Lord had given me. It doesn't take long before it all comes spiraling down when the Lord simply removes that favor and leaves us to our own devices.

As Joseph is working in Potiphar's home, indicative of the fact that he had gained great favor with Potiphar, Potiphar's wife also begins taking a special interest in Joseph. She attempts to seduce Joseph, however Joseph does the right thing and refuses her advances. When she presses him, he runs away and she fabricates a story that Joseph tried to sexually assault her, for which he is thrown in prison.

Even in his incarceration, Joseph manages to find favor with the keeper of the prison, who puts him in charge of all the other prisoners. If you're a pastor hosting a leadership conference at your church, you couldn't find a better speaker for your event than Joseph. This guy can't keep himself out of positions of leadership! Interestingly, Joseph has now been a slave for what has likely been several years. Jesus taught His disciples a seemingly counterintuitive parallel to this very concept in the New Testament.

'But Jesus called them to him and said, "You know that the rulers of the Gentiles Lord it over them, and their

—   Matthew 20:25-28

The least shall be greatest. (Luke 9:48) Whoever
would be first must be a slave. (Matthew 20:27) Humble
yourself and God will exalt you. (1Peter 5:6)

As his time in the prison continues, Joseph meets
two fellows that both fell out of rapport with Pharaoh.
The first was the chief cupbearer, and the second was the
chief baker. Both of these men have similar, yet unique
dreams that trouble them, however, Joseph is able to
interpret these dreams for each of them. The
interpretation for the chief cupbearer's dream was that in
three days, Pharaoh would restore him to his former
position as chief cupbearer. The interpretation of the
chief baker's dream was unfortunately, not one with
such a positive outcome.

*"The three baskets are three days. In three days
Pharaoh will lift up your head from you and hang you on
a tree. And the birds will eat the flesh from you."*

—   Gen. 40:18-19

Do you remember when I said that the Gospel is all over the Old Testament? This story is no exception. The chief cupbearer represents the cup, or the blood. The chief baker represents the bread, or the body.

"Now as they were eating, Jesus took bread, and after blessing it broke it and gave it to the disciples, and said, "Take, eat; this is my body." And he took a cup, and when he had given thanks he gave it to them, saying, "Drink of it, all of you, for this is my blood of the covenant, which is poured out for many for the forgiveness of sins."

    — *Matthew 26:26-28*

The baker is hung on a tree.

"The God of our fathers raised Jesus, whom you killed by hanging him on a tree."

    — *Acts 5:30*

The chief cupbearer is restored to his former position to place the cup once again in the hand of pharaoh. If you will… At his right hand?

Upon interpreting the dream of the chief cupbearer, Joseph requests one thing of him — to mention him to pharaoh. Unfortunately, the chief cupbearer forgot about Joseph for another two years until Pharaoh had a dream that troubled him. Finally, Joseph is brought out of the prison he's spent years in. He is cleaned up, shaved, and given new clothes before being brought before Pharaoh who says to him:

"I have had a dream, and there is no one who can interpret it. I have heard it said of you that when you hear a dream you can interpret it."

—   Genesis 41:15

You'd think at this point Joseph might really be trying to put his best foot forward. Perhaps try and make himself seems distinguished from everyone else so that Pharaoh might give him a job… anything but being back in that dark smelly prison. Yet Joseph's response is one of true humility that has been gleaned over years of hardships and trials.

"Joseph answered Pharaoh, "It is not in me; God will give Pharaoh a favorable answer."

— Genesis 41:16

Joseph gives all the credit to God. He doesn't try to make himself seem special or important but uses this moment before quite possibly the most powerful man in the world at the time, to give all the glory and honor to God Almighty.

After giving the interpretation regarding 7 years of abundance and 7 years of famine, Pharaoh sets Joseph apart as the most powerful man in Egypt; second only to Pharaoh himself. He uses his position to prepare for the impending famine by storing up enough grain that not only did Egypt have plenty to endure the famine, but they had enough to sell their grain to the surrounding nations.

This is when Joseph's brothers walk back onto the scene. They traveled all the way from Canaan to Egypt to buy grain and unbeknownst to them, found themselves face to face with the man they long ago had betrayed and sold as a slave. Their own flesh and blood.

Joseph then makes them go through this whole dramatic ordeal, seemingly to test where their hearts were. I think its possible that he was contemplating revenge. In his position, who wouldn't at least entertain the idea of settling the score? Yet Joseph doesn't take revenge on his brothers but gives them everything they need and even has them all relocate to Egypt with all of their families.

When he reveals to his brothers that he is Joseph, whom they sold as a slave, he says:

"And now do not be distressed or angry with yourselves because you sold me here, for God sent me before you to preserve life. For the famine has been in the land these two years, and there are yet five years in which there will be neither plowing nor harvest. And God sent me before you to preserve for you a remnant on earth, and to keep alive for you many survivors. So it was not you who sent me here, but God.

–   Genesis 45:5-8

Later on, when his father Jacob dies, his brothers start to second guess Joseph's forgiveness. They are concerned that now that their father is dead, Joseph may pay them back for what they did. They even went so far as to write Joseph a letter saying that Jacob commanded that he forgive his brothers for their sins against him. This was an outright lie. Whether or not Joseph believed the letter was authentic or not is inconsequential. What matters was his response to them:

"But Joseph said to them, "Do not fear, for am I in the place of God? As for you, you meant evil against me, but God meant it for good, to bring it about that many people should be kept alive, as they are today. So do not fear; I will provide for you and your little ones." Thus he comforted them and spoke kindly to them."

- *Genesis 50:19-21*

May we all have the attitude of Joseph towards those who have formerly wronged us.

Jesus said:

'"You have heard that it was said, "You shall love your neighbor and hate your enemy.' But I say to you, love your enemies and pray for those who persecute you,"'

- *Matthew 5:43-44*

He also gave us a strong warning against unforgiveness

"For if you forgive others their trespasses, your heavenly Father will also forgive you, but if you do not forgive others their trespasses, neither will your Father forgive your trespasses."

- *Matthew 6:14-15*

When we cling to resentment and refuse to forgive others, not only are we preventing ourselves from abiding in God's love and forgiveness, but we are showing how deep our pride continues to run. As children of God, we've been adopted through His blood sacrifice for our sins. If we truly comprehended this Gospel, we would be seeking out opportunities to forgive as we have been forgiven. The great pardon which the Almighty God has bestowed upon us should overflow in love towards our neighbors — and our enemies.

"In this is love, not that we have loved God but that he loved us and sent his Son to be the propitiation for our sins. Beloved, if God so loved us, we also ought to love one another."

    —   *1 John 4:10-11*

"We love because he first loved us. If anyone says, "I love God," and hates his brother, he is a liar; for he who does not love his brother whom he has seen cannot love God whom he has not seen. And this commandment we have from him: whoever loves God must also love his brother."

    —   *1 John 4:19-21*

Love — and forgiveness, are not optional for the Christian. John said it so clearly: If we love God we MUST love our brother.

There are certain verses & passages that I believe are grossly under-appreciated from the pulpit. One example would be Paul's warning against taking the Lord's Supper/Communion/the Eucharist in an unworthy manner. He says when one does so, they drink death upon themselves. He also says that's why so many believers have "fallen asleep" — a euphemism for having physically died. Another is this passage in Matthew 6 about unforgiveness. Let's look at Jesus' warning in verses 14-15 once more. These verses simply cannot go overlooked.

"For if you forgive others their trespasses, your heavenly Father will also forgive you, but if you do not forgive others their trespasses, neither will your Father forgive your trespasses."

Perhaps you're sitting in your bedroom or living room reading this thinking, "Okay Dan, I see what Jesus is saying, but wasn't Jesus really just speaking in superlatives to drive His point home? God knows what my father did to me. He know's what happened to me that one night. He knows I'm only human."

I don't believe so. At the very least, I certainly don't want to test that theory! And while we are indeed human, we are not merely men and women anymore. We have been born again (John 3:3). Created in Christ (Eph. 2:10). We're new creations (2Cor. 5:17). Sons & daughters of God (Gal. 4:5). Heirs with Christ (Rom. 8:17). And God's Spirit abides in each of us. (Eph. 1:13-14; 1Cor. 6:19) We mustn't ever fall back on our humanity as a means to discount the power of God over the sins and strongholds in our lives. If we do so, we certainly will never see the miraculous power of God in our lives over our vices. Sins. Addictions. Or even our lack of forgiveness.

Chapter 6

Pride & Marriage

"Therefore a man shall leave his father and mother and hold fast to his wife, and they shall become one flesh."
Genesis 2:24

A Cloudy History

Perhaps the greatest day of my life, short of the day I first sang "I have decided to follow Jesus," was the day I married my sweet wife. She and I have been together since we were teenagers and currently have 3 beautiful children together. Despite having what I would consider the most wonderful marriage, it hasn't always been smooth sailing. If anyone tells you that marriage is easy, they're lying. Much like raising children, marriage doesn't come with a manual, and many of us learned second-hand from our own parents the wrong way to live within the confines of marriage. Nevertheless, it is so incredibly rewarding.

My father was married five times. My mother was both numbers three, and five. His first wife was a girlfriend of his back when he was only 17. She was a tennis pro from England whose visa was about to expire so they got married and lived together for a brief time and then broke up.

The second was my half-sister's mother. She became pregnant in college, and they decided to do the honorable thing and get married, which didn't last long at all. What's most comical about this particular case is that right before their wedding, my father remembered that he was still legally married to his first wife. He subsequently had to track her down and get a divorce, which wasn't so simple back in 1980 prior to the internet and social media.

I wish I could say finally, but we've only made it halfway! Next was my lovely mother who met my father because her older brother was marrying my father's older sister. They tied the knot and that sweet southern-baptist woman from small-town Alabama moved to South Florida to marry my, at the time "formerly" wild and crazy alcoholic and bipolar father. About thirteen years down the road, he decides that he needs to be free again and leaves my mother. To his credit, he did stay relatively active in my life, barring a couple short stints of absence that my wife insists left me more emotionally scarred than I realize.

Oddly enough, before the ink could dry on the divorce papers, my father found himself a fourth wife who was a good bit younger than he was. Now, I still keep in touch with this woman from time to time. While the circumstances of everything were certainly less than ideal, she was actually a very kind woman with a very genuine heart. That time she spent married to my father was most certainly a low point in her life, following a divorce of her own from an abusive husband. As a matter of fact, she was on the phone with me and praying for me when I found out some pretty terrible things about my father that I don't care to divulge in this book. So, I have nothing but good things to say about her. Bless her heart, she survived being married to him!

Finally, we're back to my sweet mother! That woman endured so much emotional abuse over the 30 years that she was married to an alcoholic, bipolar, narcissist. As a matter of fact, that marriage was also all but over due in full to choices that my father made when he eventually took his own life.

Communication

Marriage is hard. According to USA Today, 41% of first marriages end in divorce. This number continues to escalate substantially with each subsequent marriage. Estimates show that 60% of second marriages and 73% of third marriages ultimately meet the same demise. I'm a big fan of country music. Generally, I like the older singers but occasionally I find a modern country artist that I like. Brad Paisley had a song on his album Fifth

Gear that is without question apropos to the conversation at hand. The chorus ended with the tagline, "If love was a plane nobody'd get on."

Consider that for just a moment. If you were booking a flight through Delta or United and they boasted a 59% successful landing rate, would you be skipping merrily by those lovely TSA agents in blue? I would certainly rather drive! Yet so many unsuspecting folks skip right down the aisle to their happily ever after that averages about 8 years.

The problem however isn't marriage. Marriage is a beautiful thing. So many people, however, are never taught how to effectively communicate with their spouse. Often times when things start to get tough a few years in, couples will go to marriage counseling to try and solve their relational problem. At times this is effective and the couple is able to work through their issues together and go on to have a long and happy life together. More often than not though, marriage counseling is too little, too late. We put the cart before the horse and wonder why we keep ending up in the ditch.

Now, I know that this isn't a book on marriage. Please bear with me though as I believe the institution of marriage exposes our deep-seated pride more clearly than the Hubble telescope.

The biggest issue that couples face in relationships is communication. This may sound like some obnoxious psychologist's ploy to get us men sitting around a table with our wives, talking about our emotions while wearing turtlenecks and sipping chamomile, but that's not at all what I'm getting at. What I'm trying to "communicate," is much simpler in nature than that. Talk to each other.

If something bothers you, say something. But don't wait until you're boiling mad over it and can't control your tongue anymore. Plenty of men and women do just that and then say, "I tried communicating and it didn't work." Of course it didn't work! This is what I like to call the "what vs. how" issue. You need to say WHAT you need to say, but HOW you say it is of equal, if not greater importance. The Apostle Paul actually taught us about this very concept.

"Rather, speaking the truth in love, we are to grow up in every way into him who is the head, into Christ,"

— *Ephesians 4:15*

This "theory" of marital communication is absolutely critical to a healthy marriage. One might even say that it is a skill that we never stop developing. Let's say hypothetically for a moment that I'm hungry but I'm also busy taking care of my overdue list of housework, so I ask my wife to make me some lunch so that I can keep making headway on my task list. I could say:

"Honey, I'm busy over here busting my butt with all this extra work you gave me, and Im starving. Could you please go make me some lunch?"

Now that's not the worst way to say that… But it certainly isn't the best either. A better alternative might be something like:

"Honey, I'm so hungry right now but I really want to keep making headway on my to-do list. Do you think you could make me something to eat so that I can keep plugging away?"

I've essentially said the same thing in both conversations, yet the second was approached with an entirely different heart and attitude. What we say and how we say it are not the only thing that matter. How we listen to our spouse is absolutely essential.

Next time you are having an argument with your spouse, ask yourself this: Am I listening to respond, or listening to understand? When we are self-absorbed and filled with pride, we listen for the sole purpose of responding so that we can one-up our spouse. On the contrary, when we are not self-seeking, but concerned more with our marriage than our own desire to be right, we will listen to our spouse to understand their heart in the matter.

Making a regular practice of checking yourself in this area will absolutely revolutionize not only your marriage, but your communication as a whole. This concept is often taught in business leadership as well because of how foundational it is to cooperative success.

Learning to consider our words is a skill in and of itself. One of my best friends, who was also the pastor that married my wife and I, gave me some great advice when my wife and I were newly engaged. He said,

"Dan, have you and Mel had a good fight yet?"

I was a bit puzzled by his question and simply responded:

"Well, no. We get along really well and don't argue much at all."

Right then he hit me with some wisdom that only a man that has been married for a good bit will understand.

"Dan, you need to go pick a fight with Mel. That may sound ridiculous, but you're going to fight at some point when your married and you need to know that the two of you can talk and work through the issue and come out on the other side together. So find something and go pick a fight with her."

I am forever grateful for those words. As it turns out, we do communicate very well and work together the way sunlight and rain do so to produce growth in a field of wildflowers, even amidst hardships & trials.

A Better Design

Christian marriages would likely take on an entirely different tone if we focused our premarital counseling more around Ephesians 5. Don't get me wrong, 1 Corinthians 13 is a beautiful passage and bursting at the seams with excellent wisdom on how to love one another. But the Apostle Paul gets much more foundational to this subject matter in Ephesians 5.

"Wives, submit to your own husbands, as to the Lord. For the husband is the head of the wife even as Christ is the head of the church, his body, and is himself its Savior. Now as the church submits to Christ, so also wives should submit in everything to their husbands. Husbands, love your wives, as Christ loved the church and gave himself up for her, that he might sanctify her, having cleansed her by the washing of water with the word, so that he might present the church to himself in splendor, without spot or wrinkle or any such thing, that she might be holy and without blemish. In the same way husbands should love their wives as their own bodies. He who loves his wife loves himself. For no one ever hated his own flesh, but nourishes and cherishes it, just as Christ does the church, because we are members of his body. "Therefore a man shall leave his father and mother and hold fast to his wife, and the two shall

become one flesh." This mystery is profound, and I am saying that it refers to Christ and the church. However, let each one of you love his wife as himself, and let the wife see that she respects her husband."

—   Ephesians 5:22-33

This passage can be a bit controversial at times depending on what side of the pendulum you swing towards regarding God's design for marriage. There are two primary views held within the Church. The first is "complementarian." This is the more traditional view that God created men and women with equal worth and value, yet inherently different, with separate gifts and skills that compliment one another so that we fit together perfectly like a jigsaw puzzle. Believers who adhere to a more complimentarian design for marriage are much more likely to believe that men and women have different "gender roles."

Alternatively, some Christians hold to an opposing viewpoint referred to as "egalitarian," or the belief that men and women, though physically different, are equal in gifts and skills that God has given them. These Christian's don't typically adhere to any specific gender roles and are typically much more open to the idea of female pastors within the Church.

My wife and I are quite traditional in our family structure and would certainly say we hold to a complementarian perspective on marriage & family. Unfortunately, many non-believers and sometimes even believers on the other end of the spectrum from us hear this and immediately think that means I as the man make all the rules, and my wife has to put her head down and submit to me. At the end of the day, if there's a direction to be taken or a decision to be make that we don't agree on and haven't been able to come to a consensus on, then yes, it falls on me. I say this because I truly hate when that happens. We make 99% of our decisions together but on rare occasion I have to make the final move, and I never do so lightly. It often makes me sick to my stomach because I don't view this as a privilege or a right, but rather a very heavy responsibility. If it fails, its on me. I think that knowing this is my heart on these rare items, gives my wife comfort in submitting to that final decision.

I don't for a minute believe that the Apostle Paul was telling women in the Church to be pushovers that never speak their minds with their husbands. Goodness gracious, if you knew my wife, you'd know she is anything but passive. She's a sweetheart. But **nobody** tells her what to do. She's a tiny ball of fire in a Laura Ingalls dress.

We sometimes have different ideas about methods in parenting and we discuss them until we have each heard one another clearly. There are things we still don't agree on today 100% that we've been talking about for years. But having been in the front row seat watching how these disagreements have unfolded, and the conversations have grown, I have also seen how each of us has begun to adopt a bit of the others perspective and we begin to naturally gravitate towards a center point together.

I believe from the deepest trenches of my soul that this can only be accomplished when each person sets aside their pride and inherent need to be right, for the good of the relationship as a whole.

Ladies, when you read those words of Paul "Wives, submit to your own husbands as to the Lord," what is your gut reaction? That initial feeling you get deep inside? If you find yourself recoiling at that word "submit," you're not alone. As a matter of fact, this was part of the curse of the fall in Genesis 3.

'To the woman he said, "I will surely multiply your pain in childbearing; in pain you shall bring forth children. ***Your desire shall be contrary to your husband, but he shall rule over you.****"'*

— Genesis 3:16

We need to be careful that we don't mistake Genesis 3:16 for a prescription of God's design for marriage. God's design was not that wife's desires would be contrary to their husbands and that the husband would rule over them. Rather, the design was clearly, though briefly, seen in the garden before the fall. God made Eve as a helper to Adam, out of his side. They were different, but they were equals. What we see in Genesis 3:16 is not a prescription but rather a description of what life will now be like after the fall. The sin that corrupted mankind wasn't eating some fruit. It was pride. The serpent told Eve that God knew that they would become "like God" if they ate of the fruit. He convinced them that God was holding out on them.

Every sin in existence today was conceived in the heart of man through one initial prideful thought. The results have been cataclysmic since that day.

So ladies, when your gut reaction to God's Word through the Apostle Paul in Ephesians 5 is to recoil at the word "submit," remember that this is the result of pride. This doesn't mean you go home, put a bonnet on and let your husband abuse you. Rather, realize that God's design is so much better than anything we could dream up.

Gentlemen, I've always thought we received the more impossible task out of the two. At the very least, it was the perfect check/balance to what Paul said to wives. It serves to offset any imbalance or inequality.

"Husbands, love your wives as Christ loved the church and gave himself up for her."

Christ's love was sacrificial. He placed His glory aside for our well-being. This means we're not out golfing on Saturdays but were home spending some much needed time with our wives. Helping her out. Giving her a break from dishes, laundry, cooking, etc. You've been at work all week and she's been home with the kids? Instead of going out with the guys, send her out with her girlfriends or to go spend some nice alone time while you watch the kids. When it's time to make a decision for the family, your wants and desires should be the last thing on the list of priorities. Our wives are our treasures and should be treated with such love and respect. If you want your wife to respect you and submit to you, try loving her like Jesus loves you.

One of my former pastor's came up with a great evangelism tool called the "three circles." It takes non-believers through a cycle that begins with the first circle: God's design. Then sin entered the world and led us to the second circle: brokenness. Our brokenness often sends us trailing off in different directions trying to find something to fix our problems and fill our voids. But when we repent and believe the Gospel (third circle), we are then able to recover and pursue the first circle again. God's Design.

The Gospel has the power to transform your marriage. We have to repent and believe though, before we can recover and pursue God's perfect design. We must repent of our pride that says, "I want it my way," if we are ever going to see God's life changing power invade and sanctify our marriages.

Public Affection

If you grew up in the 90's or early 2000's even, you've likely heard reference of "PDA," or "Public

Display of Affection." In particular, if you grew up in church going to camp or other retreats with your youth group, it's highly likely that one of the ground rules was "No Public Displays of Affection." It seems like a real buzzkill when you're 15 years old with your hormones on fire, but those rules were in place for good reason.

This was a time prior to the rise of social media as we know it today. When I was in high school, "MySpace" was still the big deal. By the time I graduated high school, Facebook was just starting to gain traction. As a matter of fact, both of my MySpace and Facebook accounts were created for me by girlfriends I had at the time.

Prior to the creation of these large social media platforms, romance as a whole was largely private by comparison. The biggest displays of affection we could find were either on the Hallmark Channel or at your local Shakespeare actors club. However, with these growing platforms came the growth in what I'll call "Public *Declarations* of Affection." This was an entirely new and unique form of PDA that was less physical in nature, and more verbal.

Every Valentines Day, Anniversary or Birthday, lovers take to their keyboards to write social media posts declaring their undying love for one another. I've certainly done this as well, so please don't take this as a prod or personal attack. What I began to realize, however, was that one romantic holiday I would see a friend post about how their husband/wife was the best and how they love that he/she is their "forever." Some of these posts were downright beautiful. They garnered hundreds of likes and comments of friends and followers that were gushing over their sweet words. Yet just a couple of months later, their profile picture changes from one of their wedding pictures to one of just them and their relationship status switches from "Married to ______," to "Single."

I watched this same thing happen, yet from a closer vantage point with one particular set of friends. As far as anyone on Facebook was concerned, my friend who I'll call Greg, was the most romantic man on the planet. He constantly showered his wife with praise and admiration in the public setting. Yet, if you spent a good deal of time with him, you'd hear an entirely different side of things. He spoke of his wife in downright awful ways. Eventually, that marriage came to a disastrous end. I can even recall him telling me about how women love to be showered with words of affection in front of everyone because it makes them feel special. While this may be true in many cases, the question we should really be asking ourselves before we push that "post" button, is: If my objective is to make my wife "feel" special, am I truly savoring her as a treasure? A great way to test this is to ask yourself if you are showing her the same affection in private as you are in public settings? This can be quite revealing of our motives.

As I sat there, a spectator to all these crumbling marriages that not so long ago seemed so strong on social media, it dawned on me that the underlying issue plaguing these relationships was that the romance and affection was not built on firm founded love that could weather any storm. A sweet facebook post isn't going to keep your marriage alive. It certainly isn't going to make your faltering relationship magically a healthy, thriving marriage. Romantic words are no substitute for a lifestyle of selfless love.

I began to get a bad taste in my mouth for the same beautifully written declarations of love which I too once penned in great fervency. First of all, I enjoyed the attention that these posts garnered. That in itself reveals the underlying motives of my heart. I chose to stop (for the most part) writing social media posts in which I declared my love for my wife, and rather, began to focus on stating these same things to her in private. I feel like my words in those moments are truer and more genuine. No one else is there to hit a like button. Nobody can comment on how sweet it is. It becomes a special moment between her and I.

Don't get me wrong, I will on rare occasion make a special post such as one for a special anniversary. One of those milestone moments. But my real declaration of love for her often happens while our children are in the living room, and we've just made coffee. Neither of us have brushed our teeth yet and we're both standing there in the kitchen getting ready to take our coffees to our perspective chairs. It's often because we're solving a problem together. Perhaps its parenting related. Sometimes I'm bouncing sermon ideas off of her or we're playfully debating a pre/post tribulation rapture.

The way we work together as a team in the day-to-day monotony will often overflow in words of affection to her: my favorite person. I hope and pray my boys find a woman like their mother one day. And I hope to God that I set the right example for my daughter as to what to look for in a husband.

You see friends, our pride and egos take one of the purest things the Lord ever created, such as the love between a man and a woman, and warp them into something wholly unrecognizable. As children of God, we should always be pursuing God's design in our lives. Prioritizing our spouse above ourselves. Resolving to serve them in all humility, especially when we don't feel like it. This means putting our pride to death every day. It boils down to choosing God's way over our own way.

Mundane Modesty

Inasmuch as marriage is not built upon great moments of valiant romance, but rather the day in and day out choices we make to work together, those day-to-day tasks can become equally destructive when not approached with the right heart.

If you've ever read the Screwtape Letters by C.S. Lewis, perhaps you know where I'm going with this. In his book, Lewis writes about deception and spiritual warfare in satirical fashion, from the perspective of none other than the devil himself. Each letter is written to the devil's nephew "Wormwood" instructing him on how to better tempt humans to sin and prevent them from repentance.

Naturally, as he writes about one temptation, he follows it up with further instructions regarding what to do if the Christian is successful in resisting the initial temptation.

This particular principle is quite visible in the modern Christian's consumption of God's Word. In that I mean that the Devil will do all he can to keep us from reading the Bible. Whether that be laws in communist countries or simply busyness and apathy in contemporary America. When we take time to read scripture however, he will then make every effort to prevent us from believing it; sowing seeds of doubt around every corner. However, if the Devil cannot prevent us from believing The Bible, he will take great pains to ensure we do not obey it or spread it to others.

As the devil will indeed do all this and more to keep us from applying God's Word to our lives, so will he do to destroy as many marriages as he can.

"The thief comes only to steal and kill and destroy. I came that they may have life and have it abundantly."

— John 10:10

In our marriage, my wife and I remained sexually pure until we were married, so the devil wasn't able to use "comparison" to cause issues as he does in many cases. Moreover, where communication is a point of major breakdown for many couples, my wife and I have typically flourished in this area. Neither of us tends to get overly emotional in our problem solving, so we generally approach disagreements from very logical positions and state our positions and feelings until we both understand each other. As a result, nearly every argument we've had has ended with us realizing that one of us misunderstood something the other was saying. So, we both laugh, hug and carry on with the day.

The biggest area where the devil was able to steal, kill, and destroy, came in the form of mundane housework. I grew up in a home in which my mother kept everything perfectly tidy. Everything had a place. If there was an ounce of clutter, she performed recon, infiltrated, and eliminated the target like Seal Team 6. My wife on the other hand grew up in a home that was a bit different. Our perception on what was acceptable was very different. This led to quite a few arguments in the early years of our marriage. In her defense, I am a bit OCD.

This discrepancy in what we both could live with usually came to a climax with me angrily cleaning the house. Imagine if you were to combine the Incredible Hulk and the quintessential 1950's housewife. Apron and all. That was me.

I would obsessively clean and reorganize everything in the house as if working in fast-forward until I was ready to collapse in exhaustion. But not until I expressed my great dissatisfaction with what the amount of work I had to do by myself. Mind you, I typically did this when I was home alone, so its not as if my wife even had the chance to help. I would clean and organize in an absolute rage.

After years of praying for this situation to change with little tangible difference, something finally happened! The Holy Spirit began convicting me of my own sin relating to this issue. He began throwing up red flags in my mind every time I had a prideful thought. Each time I said to myself:

"I shouldn't have to do all this myself!"

"This isn't fair!" or,

"She doesn't appreciate everything I do for her,"

He would hit me with conviction like a bag of bricks.

Eventually, those convicting "red flags" turned into something much more foundational. The Lord helped me to trade my pride fueled anger for gratitude.

I began to be thankful that I had a wife who loved me as she did and was the best mother to our babies. I became grateful for the dishes to do because that meant we had food on the table. I grew to be joyful when cleaning the house because we had a house to clean. So many in our world are lacking the bare essentials. Those of us in first world countries have ample reasons to be thankful. Gratitude is a great weapon against our pride. Our beloved Baptist Hymnal has one of my favorite songs about gratitude:

When upon life's billows you are tempest tossed,

When you are discouraged, thinking all is lost,

Count your many blessings, name them one by one,

And it will surprise you what the Lord hath done.

Are you ever burdened with a load of cares?

Does the cross seem heavy you are called to bear?

Count your many blessings, every doubt will fly,

And you will be singing as the days go by.

When you look at others with their lands and gold,

Think that Christ has promised you His wealth untold;

Count your many blessings, money cannot buy

Your reward in heaven, nor your home on high.

So, amid the conflict, whether great or small,

Do not be discouraged, God is over all;

Count your many blessings, angels will attend,

Help and comfort give you to your journey's end."

(Count Your Blessings, Johnson Oatman Jr.
1897)

Chapter 7

Pride & Parenting

*"Fathers, do not provoke your children to anger, but bring them up in the
discipline and instruction of the Lord."*
Ephesians 6:4

Priorities

President Theodore Roosevelt once said,
"Nothing in the world is worth having or worth doing
unless it means effort, pain, difficulty."

Quite possibly the most challenging endeavor I
have ever undertaken is being a father. Parenthood is not
for the weak-minded. Perhaps this is a contributing
factor to the high rate of fatherless homes and abortions.
Even before becoming a parent, many are well aware of
the obstacles ahead and therefore opt never to even risk
the possibility.

I recently read an excerpt on a corresponding topic from a retired Green Beret. If you're familiar at all with our military's special operations units, you'll know that Green Beret's are the U.S. Army's elite fighting force, aside from perhaps Delta Force. They endure grueling selection processes designed to test not only their physical capabilities, but the strength of each individual's will to succeed. It truly takes a special kind of person to persevere through these weeks long courses, that involves everything from intense physical training to lack of food and sleep deprivation. Even the fittest of soldiers often bow out because these cumulative challenges are simply too much to bear at once.

The aforementioned Green Beret retiree, now a husband and father said,

"Earning my green beret was easy… The hardest part of my life was trying to convince the guy that earned that beret that it means nothing if your heart isn't full. Men will go to crazy lengths to prove themselves right. That we can do whatever we want if we put our minds to it. We're tougher. We're built differently. So we bury our emotions and we grind things into a pulp if that's what it takes. Our bodies break. Spirits get crushed. We will take it to the limit just to win. And then what? Once we win… Once we're the champion… Once we get the job, the tab, the wings, the contract, the house, the truck, the title, the recognition, the honor, the fulfillment for the moment… Then what? No one talks about who's left when the dust of the world settles around us… See all

those are just things. They don't change a man's heart.
They callous it."

-Adam Free

All too often we grow fixated on the next
milestone in our lives. Please don't misunderstand me:
Goals are great. Ask any highly successful person in
virtually any field how they managed to attain the
position they're currently in and they'll almost certainly
bring up the goals they set for themselves. Business
leadership coaches will tell you to set long and short-
term goals to help you measure your success periodically
as you continue to drive forward. But who's standing in
the dust as you drive down the road to a better job? That
promotion? That car? That boat?

Sadly, our families all too often get the brunt end
of our efforts. And when they speak or act from their
deprivation of time, attention and affection, we react out
of our inflated egos.

"How dare they speak to me like that!"

"Don't they know what I do for this family?"

"I bust my butt to provide for everyone!"

"I deserve some respect!"

There may be a good deal of truth in the previous statements. More often than not however, sin doesn't present itself as a blatant lie. It comes disguised in truth and logic yet twists the heart until the truth is no longer recognizable. I know I've certainly let each of those thoughts run around my head like an angry chihuahua. Yet, when I step back and ponder the greatness of God for a moment, I realize that in my pride, I've become like that ridiculous little dog, barking at King Kong.

Perhaps the single most lethal attack to one's ego is not found in cleverly crafted comments designed to take them down a notch. No. The greatest killer of one's pride is beholding the supremacy of God for himself in light of his own feeble frame. This is indeed sanctifying.

Jon Piper once said, "Man was made for mountains. Not mirrors."

We were created to walk in harmony with Almighty God. Yet, when our sin separated us from Him, we got exactly what Adam and Eve were looking for. We became "like" God. Or more appropriately, we became our own gods, and the world spiraled into utter chaos and depravity. If we do not now make a conscious effort to put the prideful man to death and in turn dwell on the Author of life, we will merely continue tumbling downhill into absolute ruin. And who are we dragging along with us? Our spouses? Our children?

But God…

Parenting is indeed, hard. As a father I go to work and come home exhausted day after day. We are burdened by finances, marital issues, health problem, vehicles breaking down, etc. And at the end of each day, our children want the world from us. They need our time and attention; our every last drop of energy. And despite our greatest efforts to provide for their every physical, mental, and spiritual need, they still have the audacity at times to forget about it all and speak to us as if we haven't given them everything that they possess. The similarities of this and how we treat our Heavenly Father are too close for comfort.

I can recall a brief encounter with my oldest son one rainy day at home. He's sitting at the table doing his schoolwork for the day while I'm in the downstairs bathroom that I just did hours worth of repairs and cleaning in. I look down and see toilet paper and water all over the floor and more toilet paper laying in the dog's water dish. It was really the timing of this more than anything that set me off because this certainly wasn't the first time I'd seen a mess similar to this one. Therefore, I shouted from the bathroom:

"Kids! Why is there toilet paper in the dog's water dish?"

My son replies from the dining room table:

"Sorry!"

Then he continues…

"Daddy, can you not shout while I'm doing my school?"

Not the time son. The ill-timing of his response definitely had my teapot whistling. I wanted to march right into the dining room in my typical drill-sergeant fashion and teach him a lesson about back-talking me like that. I grew up in the South and was raised with extremely high standards for respect and manners. Moreover, disrespect is not tolerated in our home either. The use of "sir" and "ma'am" are not optional. In fact, my wife and I even refer to each other as sir and ma'am out of respect for one another.

In this moment, however, when I stepped back and took a deep breath, I knew intrinsically that he wasn't backtalking or being intentionally disrespectful. He was simply trying to communicate with me and the only thing it hurt was my own pride. How we respond to our children matters because they grow up to emulate us. If we insist that they speak respectfully to us as their parents and other adults, are we in turn speaking respectfully to our spouse? Moreover, are we speaking to our children with the same respect that we expect from them?

Please don't misunderstand me: I believe there should be a clear delineation between parent & child. They need to know who the authority figure is and what the expectations are of them. However, when I was first challenged to consider this idea of speaking to my children with the same respect that I expected from them, it was as if someone were following me around poking me with a pitchfork at every turn. The more I realized how hypocritical I had been in my expectations for my beloved little ones, the stronger my conviction regarding this matter grew.

Ideally, all of us parents would love to be picture perfect with how we raise and nurture our children. We'd love to be modern day Ward & June Cleaver's. Unfortunately, much like in the case of marriage, many of us didn't grow up with the best examples to follow. Unless we dive into the deep waters of introspection, many of us may never come to understand why we say or do certain things with our children. This principle applies to just about every facet of our lives.

For instance, let's just say for a moment that you are out at the mall doing some shopping when one of your children throws a bit of a fit in public. I realize that this is a far-fetched scenario. Who's ever heard of a kid throwing a fit in a store? As parents, its our job to respond to this situation and handle it as best as we know how. Different people choose different methods of parenting and discipline for a variety of reasons, and I'm certainly not here to tell you what I think you should do. This same scenario happened with myself when I was just a wee lad at K-Mart with my mother. I wanted something and she said no. So, I wailed about it. It was the first and last time that ever happened. I can still remember the color of the bathroom floor that I was staring at while my rear end was tanned like a deer hide. I have had to do the same thing with my own children. I take no issue with that method of discipline, so long as it is done in self-control and not from anger. How we discipline isn't the issue that I want to address. Why we discipline is an entirely different situation. Our motives are foundational to the principles we build upon them.

Why are we disciplining our children in the aforementioned scenario? Is it to teach them appropriate behavior in public? Fantastic. Is it perhaps because their wailing has disrupted everyone else's time shopping, and you want to teach them to be considerate of others? Wonderful! Is it because they made you as a parent look bad in public?

I remember the first time I heard that question posed to me. You could hear the crickets. But they (my wife) were right. We should never punish our children for the reason that they made us look bad. This is nothing more than reinforcing our own pride with our circumstantial authority. This scenario is summarized quite well in one of the many parables that Jesus told:

"Can a blind man lead a blind man? Will they not both fall into a pit? A disciple is not above his teacher, but everyone when he is fully trained will be like his teacher. Why do you see the speck that is in your brother's eye, but do not notice the log that is in your own eye? How can you say to your brother, 'Brother, let me take out the speck that is in your eye,' when you yourself do not see the log that is in your own eye? You hypocrite, first take the log out of your own eye, and then you will see clearly to take out the speck that is in your brother's eye."

– Luke 6:39-42

We may indeed still need to discipline our children for other reasons in a moment when they've also just made us look bad. They've injured our pride. Good. Now that our pride is injured, let's kill it while its weak. As John Owen said, "Be killing sin or sin will be killing you."

The heart behind our discipline is of far more importance than the method in which we carry it out. If we want our children to grow up to know and love the Lord, we need first to put aside ourselves. We have expectations for our children. But what is the source of those expectations? Is it God's Word? Or is it the glory/shame we receive when they behave a certain way?

"For the one who sows to his own flesh will from the flesh reap corruption, but the one who sows to the Spirit will from the Spirit reap eternal life."
       — *Galatians 6:8*

When our discipline is sewn from our flesh, we reap corrupted children. However, when our discipline is sewn from the leading of the Holy Spirit, we introduce our children to the one who offers eternal life, and transformation through a renewed mind.

A parent's pride in discipline can have devastating eternal consequences. The last thing we want is to be a hinderance in the way of our children and a relationship with the Lord. We certainly do not want to be like Jesus' disciples who thought He was too important for the people to bring their children to.

"And they were bringing children to him that he might touch them, and the disciples rebuked them. But when Jesus saw it, he was indignant and said to them, "Let the children come to me; do not hinder them, for to such belongs the kingdom of God."

       — *Mark 10:13-14*

We are the shepherds of our children's hearts. We cannot simply take them to church, drop them off and expect the responsibility of their spiritual well-being to somehow bypass us. We ought to take great care to ensure that our own sins, such as our pride, do not serve to construct walls between our little ones and faith in Christ.

Chapter 8

Pride in Ministry

"Woe to the shepherds who destroy and scatter the sheep of my pasture!"
Jeremiah 23:1

Pastor Mark Driscoll has been one of the leading voices in the American evangelical church for over two decades. He founded Mars Hill Church in Seattle Washington back in 1996 and pastored its congregation for nearly twenty years until his resignation in 2014.

I personally was a big fan of his sermons and had quite a few on my iPod that I would listen to while driving around delivering orders for Chick Fil A back in college. Needless to say, I was pretty saddened to hear about his resignation in 2014 and the occasion for this sudden transition.

Some of the various reasons that were cited in the wake of Pastor Mark's sudden resignation included issues with pride, anger, and a "domineering spirit."

Unfortunately, as a result, the Mars Hills church network dissolved shortly after in 2015. A great deal of church members were left either hurt or confused in the settling dust of everything that transpired.

I can guarantee you that Pastor Mark is not the only pastor to have dealt with these issues. This doesn't excuse his actions, but we also must bear in mind that as the Church, our first response to sin in a brother should be grace and forgiveness, as we have all received. There may need to be tangible repercussions for the sake of Christ's beloved Church, but these men & women are still brothers and sisters.

"For if you forgive others their trespasses, your heavenly Father will also forgive you, but if you do not forgive others their trespasses, neither will your Father forgive your trespasses."

—   Matthew 6:14-15

Amends

When I was a young man, I experienced a similar encounter with a pastor at the church I grew up in. Now, this was not the lead pastor, or anyone very well known outside of this relatively large church. I still have a great love for this church and the work they did and still continue to do. Nevertheless, the church had a music minister that had a reputation for being incredibly arrogant and treating church employees very poorly. For the sake of anonymity, I will call him Bill. I can recall listening to him berate the church's sound guys and pro-presenter operators if anything was not working absolutely perfectly. If you've ever been involved in church music ministry, then you will be keenly aware of how common these technical issues are and how they are generally nobody's fault. Often times it was because either someone's computer had a new update that automatically changed various settings, or the computer really needed an update.

Singers as a whole have a reputation for being divas. Church singers are no exception to this unfortunate stereotype. On my end, as an electric guitar player, we are notoriously OCD. God forbid anything be going on with my gear or messing with my guitars tone. I would lose my ever-loving mind.

On another occasion, this same individual, Bill, was going to carpool with another pastor at our church, who I'll call Smith, from one campus to another. Smith was quite the comedian, and while attempting to joke with him, Bill stopped his car in the church parking lot and told Smith to get out and find his own ride.

Now, I worked relatively closely with Smith for several years and grew to really love that guy. As with any of us, he had his moments of "human reactions," however one of these moments was actually something I never forgot. In the heat of pre-service preparation with various last-minute changes and technical issues, I was hanging around with another young man in the sound booth which was quite the tight space. In his frustration with everything go on, Smith, in a rather brash tone, told myself and the other young man to get out of the sound booth. It was nothing major, though I was a little annoyed in the moment. However, after service Smith made a point of finding me and apologizing for his words. And I truly felt that his apology was genuine. That is a man I can respect. I never saw this kind of repentance from Bill towards those whom he spoke poorly to.

Previously, I mentioned my time working at Chick Fil A. The General Manager during my time there taught me a good deal as a young man. Quite possibly the most valuable lesson he taught me was about personal responsibility. I will call him Joe. You may be wondering why I've included a story about Chick fil A in a chapter on ministry, however, Joe didn't just view his job at our store as selling chicken. He was constantly evangelizing and discipling us teenagers who worked for him. At times he could be a bit brash. Sometimes he needed to be. One instance in particular, I can recall him sending me to the back of the store to restock a list of items for the front of house. I was back there working away when apparently, the lunch rush had arrived. Joe came running to the back and hollered at me, "Dan! There's a sea of people up here! Get down and get on register!"

I remember this moment being an exercise in self control and submission for me. I was doing exactly as I had been told, and doing so diligently. So being chastised in that moment truly agitated me and activated my own prideful thoughts.

"How dare he!"

"The nerve of this guy!"

Yet, when that lunch rush passed and everything at the store settled down, Joe came to me and sincerely apologized for what he had said to me. All at once, my own pride was disarmed, and I learned yet again a life lesson that is truly priceless.

We all make mistakes. We act out in our stress and emotions and hurt others. How we proceed from there is what defines a large portion of our character. We can ignore our destructive behavior, pretending it never happened and acting all "buddy-buddy" with the person we've just wounded. We can deflect from our own personal responsibility and blame them for whatever we believe was the cause of our harmful behavior. This is what narcissists typically do. However there remains a third and supremely better option. Humility.

Now, humility isn't an apology followed by a "but." If you ever catch yourself saying "I'm sorry, but…" You're not really sorry. In fact, for lack of a better phrase, you're full of yourself. You need to get your "but" out of the way."

Apologizing isn't simply an act of repentance. It's a skill we develop. Or rather, it develops us. When we first begin practicing getting our "but" out of the way, we might only be able to muster the words "I'm sorry," as it takes all of our mental faculties to resist the urge to say "but you…" However, as time goes on and we make a habit of humbling ourselves, we should see our apologies progress from a simple "I'm sorry," to "Im sorry for how I acted," to "Im so sorry for how I acted. I never meant to hurt you, but I did, and I hope you can forgive me."

Furthermore, saying "I'm sorry that you were offended by what I said," is also not a genuine apology. That statement is nothing more than a thinly veiled avoidance of any personal responsibility. This was my father's go-to "apology," or shall I say, "damage control."

Shepherds

When men and women in positions of ministry allow their egos to go unchecked, the results are disastrous. When the man called to pastor a congregation begins to think too highly of himself, his congregants will inevitably be left in the dark like a sheep without a shepherd. That is, in fact, what a pastor is: a shepherd.

The Greek noun utilized for "pastor" by the Apostle Paul in Ephesians 4:11 when he lists the "fivefold gifts" of the Holy Spirit, is "poimēn." This word translates very literally to our word for "shepherd." It was later translated to "Pastor" in the Latin Vulgate, the translation utilized by much of the Church for centuries until the Protestant Reformation. This Latin word "Pastor" is still in common usage today in languages such as Spanish, Portuguese & Italian. And it still means shepherd.

I remember when I first decided I was going to learn Spanish and was therefore attending a Latin-American church in South Florida. I really do miss that group of believers. One Sunday night though, I remember the Pastor preaching a sermon on the "Buen Pastor," or "Good Pastor." I kept thinking to myself, "Man this guy has a lot to say about himself." Then it dawned on me… He wasn't talking about himself. He was quoting John 10.

"I am the good shepherd. The good shepherd lays down his life for the sheep. He who is a hired hand and not a shepherd, who does not own the sheep, sees the wolf coming and leaves the sheep and flees, and the wolf snatches them and scatters them. He flees because he is a hired hand and cares nothing for the sheep. I am the good shepherd. I know my own and my own know me..."

–   John 10:11-14

Pastors have an obligation to their congregation. It may be more appropriate for us to switch to the terminology that Jesus used. Shepherds have an obligation to their flock. To guide them and protect them. To set aside their own comforts for the well being of their sheep. Any diligent shepherd is going to smell like his sheep. He'll end up covered in the same mud as his sheep. When it rains on them, it rains on him. In fact, if they've been out in the field long enough, they probably won't have trimmed their beard in quite some time and might even start to look like a sheep!

One of Jesus' more famous teachings was the parable of the lost sheep.

"What man of you, having a hundred sheep, if he has lost one of them, does not leave the ninety-nine in the open country, and go after the one that is lost, until he finds it? And when he has found it, he lays it on his shoulders, rejoicing. And when he comes home, he calls together his friends and his neighbors, saying to them, 'Rejoice with me, for I have found my sheep that was

*lost.' Just so, I tell you, there will be more joy in heaven
over one sinner who repents than over ninety-nine
righteous persons who need no repentance."*

–   Luke 15:4-7

I believe the overarching motif in this parable is
evangelistic in nature. By that I mean that Jesus is
clearly talking about a sinner repenting and coming
home, much like the story of the prodigal son.
Personally, I'm not one to say that the same passage of
scripture can say two different things to two different
people. That borderlines on relativism, which espouses
the lie that there is no objective truth, but rather, all truth
is relative. You may have heard someone say, "That may
be your truth, but this is my truth." Or "All religions are
really just different avenues to the same God." Run away
from that methodology of thinking. This is a deceptive
lie that has led many sheep astray. However, I do think
at times, there are passages that may give us greater
insight and perspective based on the vantage point we
are reading from. So while this parable of the lost sheep
is clearly about a sinner returning to the Lord, Pastors
might garner a bit more out of the details simply based
on their unique perspective. Remember, a pastor is a
shepherd. So, if we approach this passage from the
perspective of shepherding church members, we may
learn an extra thing or two from the "Good Shepherd"
himself.

Notice first that this shepherd in the parable
notices that one of his sheep has gone astray. He is

diligent. He isn't oblivious to the fact that he's missing one out of a hundred. This means he's keeping track of his flock and paying attention to where they're at. Then, upon noticing that he is missing a sheep, he leaves the comfort of the flock to go out into the wilderness to find it. He doesn't simply say "Well good riddance! That sheep was always a pain to deal with anyways." We certainly have church members that fit that bill! After finding his lost sheep, the shepherd then throws it over his shoulders and carries it home. When we find a strayed church member, do we take the same pains to bring them home as the shepherd in this parable? We invite them home. Are they hurt? Too tired and weary from their lost journey to make it back on their own? We ought to follow the Good Shepherd's lead and throw them over our shoulders and bring them home. Not to shame. But to rejoicing! The friends & neighbors here in Luke 15 are our fellow church members. The return of a strayed church member should be cause for great rejoicing.

On the contrary, if that shepherd is too concerned with his own well being, he won't be able to satisfy the duties of his job.

Similarly, when pastors become consumed by their own visions, they begin to look at their congregants less like sheep to shepherd, and more like pawns on their chess board. However, Jesus gave us the perfect example to follow.

"Come to me, all who labor and are heavy laden, and I will give you rest. Take my yoke upon you, and learn from me, for I am gentle and lowly in heart, and you will find rest for your souls. For my yoke is easy, and my burden is light."

— *Matthew 11:28-30*

If the Matchless One… The King of Kings… Lord of Lords… Ancient of Day… If He is gentle and lowly in heart, then how dare we be anything different. This is the big issue I take with the overarching theme of "leadership" in the Church. I cannot tell you how many leadership conferences/meetings I've been to in various churches. I don't believe that the idea of helping to better equip leaders within the church is a bad thing. However, when "leadership" takes the place of being a servant, it needs to go.

Do you have any idea how many times Jesus talked about leadership in the Gospels? Zero. Not one single time. In fact, Jesus' message to his twelve disciples was quite contrary to much of the verbiage regurgitated by leadership gurus at many of our church conferences.

One such occasion was when James & John, the sons of Zebedee came to Jesus asking Him to let them sit at his right and left hands in His glory. These two knuckleheads were ironically enough, also referred to as the "sons of thunder." I think this may have had something to do with their tempers and overall bullheadedness. In this moment, the other disciples weren't overly thrilled with their request to Jesus. His response, however, has been the theme of countless sermons and books ever since.

'And Jesus called them to him and said to them, "You know that those who are considered rulers of the Gentiles Lord it over them, and their great ones exercise authority over them. But it shall not be so among you. But whoever would be great among you must be your servant, and whoever would be first among you must be slave of all. For even the Son of Man came not to be served but to serve, and to give his life as a ransom for many."'

—   Mark 10:42-45

Unfortunately, some church members find themselves in a situation where they have a pastor who is constantly beating the drum that says congregants have to submit to his authority as their pastor. Now, as church members we should submit to our pastor's leadership in the Church. He is in fact the shepherd that God has in our lives to help lead and guide us. However, when a pastor lets their own ego, or even insecurities take the wheel of their hearts, they often go down this dangerous road in which they begin to have a "my way or the highway" attitude. Such attitudes have no place in

Church leadership. Many churches have fallen apart due to one man's attitude being of this nature.

The only one that merits this type of attitude is God Himself. And while the reality of our situation is that it is indeed His way, or the "highway to hell," this isn't the attitude with which He treats His own.

Do you remember earlier when we to looked at the transformation of the Apostle Peter? We saw him humbled greatly in just a few short chapters. Yet when Jesus restored Peter — that moment on the shore after the resurrection when He asked Peter three times if Peter loved him — what was Jesus doing? He was cooking breakfast for his disciples! He was serving them.

"Just as day was breaking, Jesus stood on the shore; yet the disciples did not know that it was Jesus. Jesus said to them, "Children, do you have any fish?" They answered him, "No." He said to them, "Cast the net on the right side of the boat, and you will find some." So they cast it, and now they were not able to haul it in, because of the quantity of fish. That disciple whom Jesus loved therefore said to Peter, "It is the Lord!" When Simon Peter heard that it was the Lord, he put on his outer garment, for he was stripped for work, and threw himself into the sea. The other disciples came in the boat, dragging the net full of fish, for they were not far from the land, but about a hundred yards off. When they got out on land, they saw a charcoal fire in place, with fish laid out on it, and bread. Jesus said to them, "Bring some of the fish that you have just caught." So Simon

What a simple, yet beautiful picture of how we ought to prostrate our hearts, not simply before our God, but also our brothers. All to often though we miss the mark on what being sanctified really looks like. Is it better behavior? Sometimes. Is it when we stop cursing? That's all well & good. The vast majority of our sanctification, however, happens when we lay down our pride, and take upon ourselves the character which Christ Jesus so purely displayed throughout His life, that we find in His Word.

Please don't miss this! In the previously stated story from the twenty-first chapter of The Gospel of John, we are no longer looking at simply the Messiah, come to earth to offer salvation to mankind. No. This is the **risen** Savior! He already paid the price of our sins, walked out of the tomb, and is about to ascend to heaven and sit down at the right hand of God the Father. And where do we find him? Stoking a charcoal fire and roasting some fish for a bunch of guys who were too chicken to show up to his execution. If that doesn't change the perspective of your heart, then I'm not sure what will.

If Almighty God can act in such simple humility when He has just carried out the greatest victory in the history of creation, we too can humble ourselves. We **must** humble ourselves. This example of "leadership," if you will, has been at the core of Chick Fil A corporate training for decades. It's called "Servant Leadership."

This example that Jesus set for us in John is one that those of us in ministry need to take to heart even more so than our brothers and sisters who aren't in direct ministerial roles. Rich Wilkerson reinforced this well when he said, "If you're too big to serve, you're too small to lead."

There is perhaps one even greater example of this servant leadership portrayed in scripture. Before the Passover Feast in John 13, Jesus does something that still to this day leaves me stunned.

"During supper, when the devil had already put it into the heart of Judas Iscariot, Simon's son, to betray him, Jesus, knowing that the Father had given all things into his hands, and that he had come from God and was going back to God, rose from supper. He laid aside his outer garments, and taking a towel, tied it around his waist. Then he poured water into a basin and began to

*wash the disciples' feet and to wipe them with the towel
that was wrapped around him."*

   –   John 13:2-5

*"When he had washed their feet and put on his outer
garments and resumed his place, he said to them, "Do
you understand what I have done to you? You call me
Teacher and Lord, and you are right, for so I am. If I
then, your Lord and Teacher, have washed your feet, you
also ought to wash one another's feet. For I have given
you an example, that you also should do just as I have
done to you. Truly, truly, I say to you, a servant is not
greater than his master, nor is a messenger greater than
the one who sent him. If you know these things, blessed
are you if you do them."*

   –   John 13:12-17

There are quite a few details that we can garner
from this passage. The first thing that seems to be
glaring in our face is the fact that Judas was already
planning to betray Jesus. And Jesus knew! Yet He chose
to wash his feet anyway. Some may question whether or
not Judas was there for the foot washing, however, the
fact that he is still present in verses 21-30 is indicative of
the fact that he was indeed present for this special
moment.

Secondly, Jesus strips off his outer garment, and wraps a towel around his waist. This was historically speaking, the job of the lowest servant on the "totem pole" if you will. Consider the setting for a moment. These guys have been traveling around all over Israel following Jesus and preaching the Gospel that they still don't understand. Most of the roads are dirt. This is an agricultural society so there are animals everywhere, and with animals comes "excrement." Let's not forget that these guys are all wearing sandals too. These had to be some truly nasty feet. Yet here we have… **God**… humbling Himself to the position of the lowest servant, in order to serve his friends and followers, and teach them that His ways are indeed higher than ours, as He said to the prophet Isaiah.

"For my thoughts are not your thoughts, neither are your ways my ways, declares the Lord. For as the heavens are higher than the earth, so are my ways higher than your ways and my thoughts than your thoughts."

–   Isaiah 55:8-9

The key point that Jesus is trying to drive home here is humility. He knows that the His disciples will be taken aback by this gesture. Peter tried even to refuse because he knew how backwards this was.

Finally, Jesus leaves His disciples with a charge.

"If I then, your Lord and Teacher, have washed your feet, you also ought to wash one another's feet... If you know these things, blessed are you if you do them."

Notice that Jesus doesn't say, "Blessed are you if you know these things." No. This blessing is conditional. "IF you know these things, blessed are you IF YOU DO THEM." I wonder if James was thinking about this when he wrote the words "Faith without works is dead."

So, what does this mean then for pastors and ministry leaders? Well, the truths here that Jesus teaches us are very much so objective. However, the application in each individual circumstance is going to be subjective.

I previously mentioned a pastor that I called Smith. Smith was my youth pastor in middle school, and I served as a student leader under him while in high school. I remember one particular day after service seeing Smith picking up trash that was laying around and sweeping the floor. Now, this was a very large church with facility workers who would come in to clean up each day. Yet here he is, taking off his pastor hat. And throwing on the janitor's garb. I am truly grateful for this example. In fact, the other day I was preaching at a Senior Adult Revival, where both my mother and grandmother were as well. After preaching the message on the joy of the Lord where I attempted to get these older believers fired up about the Lord, we had lunch together. I sat at a round table with my grandmother and her friends while we joked about some of the passages from my sermon involving David & Bathsheba. I'll let your imagination fill in the blanks. When we all finished eating, I took everyone plates and stacked them up before carrying them to the trash can. In that moment I immediately thought of the example that Smith set for me as a young teenager.

Who cares if you're the preacher. Honestly, you may be able to preach the best message ever spoken from that pulpit, but if you aren't humble enough to turn around and serve those you just preached to, you need to find another job.

Our church has a good size food ministry that serves our community. This ministry "Manna Ministries," passes out food to residents in need at various "food drops" throughout the month, and also has a "community dinner" once a month at the church. There are a handful of older ladies including my mother who make this ministry function. They are serving their hearts out in the church kitchen for nothing but treasure in heaven. So what can we as pastors, preachers, ministers etc. do to be like Jesus and serve them? They will never turn down an extra set of hands to help with dishes, sweep the floor, and wipe down tables.

We also need to bear in mind that we aren't doing this for the recognition of anyone but the Lord Himself. In fact, Jesus gave us yet another example of doing "spiritual things" with the wrong heart.

The first church I ever had a regular preaching engagement at was this small country church in rural Alabama. When I say small, I mean I had more children than they had members who came to church. My family more than doubled the size of the congregation each Sunday. The sweet older lady who coordinated everything for their church would often apologize for them not having more people. I think she understood the work that went into preparing those sermons and felt bad that there weren't more people there to hear the messages. Now, were I my younger self, I may have been tempted to think "This isn't worth my time." Or "God called me to teach the Word. How can I do that when only two people show up for church?"

The answer is faithfully. If you are a pastor/teacher, you were called to preach the Word of God faithfully. He likely never told you how many people to preach to. So, whether you're preaching to two or two thousand, do it faithfully with your whole heart. This really boils down to the parable of the talents in Matthew 25.

"For it will be like a man going on a journey, who called his servants and entrusted to them his property. To one he gave five talents, to another two, to another one, to each according to his ability. Then he went away. He who had received the five talents went at once and traded with them, and he made five talents more. So also he who had the two talents made two talents more. But he who had received the one talent went and dug in the ground and hid his master's money. Now after a long time the master of those servants came and settled accounts with them. And he who had received the five talents came forward, bringing five talents more, saying, 'Master, you delivered to me five talents; here, I have made five talents more.' His master said to him, 'Well done, good and faithful servant. You have been faithful

–   *Matthew 25:14-21*

One thing we don't see in this parable is the servants acting in their own interests. In fact, the only one that did was the one who was ultimately rejected by the master later in the passage. There are a variety of ways in which we let ourselves get in the way of the work that God wants to do in and through us. One of these is an inflated perspective of our own importance. Never forget this: God doesn't need you. You are not a crucial part of His work. Rather, He has given us the opportunity to take part in His incredible works as willing vessels. Don't think for a minute that you are integral to His working. I have seen this in a number of men and women whom The Lord has placed a message in their hearts to share.

My father was one such person. He had a strong passion for God's grace to the "least of these." What plagued him however was that in his own narcissism, he became convinced that he himself was integral to this message. He had the misconception that he was the only one preaching the message of God's grace to alcoholics, drug addicts, the homeless and other Odd Todds. Often times this convoluted view came out in hostility towards God's Church, which is something we all need to be weary of. After all, the Church is Christ's Bride. I know how I feel any time I've heard someone speak negatively of my wife. It would be ill-advised to speak poorly of God's wife.

Another way in which this inflated view of self-importance in ministry can be seen is when pastors/ministers regularly push others to listen to their message, as if to say, "I have something important to say!" Now, at times God has warned His people in such ways through prophets, and I do believe He still does. That doesn't mean however, that these men and women are immune to becoming arrogant with their God-given message.

Once again, my father was the king of this. He also loved to write, and whenever he did, he would send his writings to anyone he could find to read them. It became less about sharing God's Word and more about saying "Look how spiritual I am!" Admittedly, when I was younger, I did the same thing. When the Holy Spirit convicted me of this, I ran away from anything that would draw attention to myself in this way. It was a good number of years before I felt like the Holy Spirit gave me the green light to start practicing the gifts that He had given me. I'm by no means excusing myself for years of inactivity in ministry. However, we ourselves cannot effectively minister if this work is not preceded by our own personal repentance.

Chapter 9

Good News

"For our sake he made him to be sin who knew no sin, so that in him we might become the righteousness of God."
2 Corinthians 5:21

In 1987, my grandfather suddenly passed away from what the doctors determined was a massive heart attack. At only 54 years old, our family was completely caught off guard by his sudden death. He seemed to be the picture of health for a man his age with no apparent health issues. Then again, this is often the case with heart disease. Not everyone suffering from a weak or damaged heart is morbidly obese or carrying around an oxygen tank. He was a hard-working man, beloved by his family & friends, and in a moment gone.

As ailments such as heart disease, strokes and aneurisms can in but a moment reveal the true state of a man's health, so the underlying depravity of his heart will be revealed on judgement day. Jesus said it this way:

"Not everyone who says to me, 'Lord, Lord,' will enter the kingdom of heaven, but the one who does the will of my Father who is in heaven. On that day many will say to me, 'Lord, Lord, did we not prophesy in your name, and cast out demons in your name, and do many mighty works in your name?' And then will I declare to them, 'I never knew you; depart from me, you workers of lawlessness.'"

— Matthew 7:21-23

What I find the most interesting and simultaneously terrifying in this passage is the fact that these individuals are calling Jesus "Lord." They are even falling back on the various works that they've done in His name for the Kingdom. This makes me think of a number of prosperity gospel preachers and televangelists who supposedly heal people and cast out demons on a regular basis. Now, I am not a cessationist, and therefore believe that all of the spiritual gifts spoken of in the New Testament are still active today. And while some men & women certainly falsify these gifts, I think a number of these genuinely believe in what they're doing, as do many of us in our perspective ministries. Nevertheless, we all need to take Jesus' warning with the utmost sincerity.

If our work in ministry serves to bolster our own feelings of self-worth and egos, we may very well find ourselves in the position of those Jesus spoke of in the aforementioned passage. On the contrary, if we humble ourselves and seek not our own elevation but the glory of our God & King, there is no limitation to what He can accomplish through us with prostrate hearts.

The Bible gives us a number of warnings against pride and arrogance. Many of these we have already looked at. However, as every one of us looks in the mirror each morning to adjust our appearance as we get ready for the day, so too we ought to look in God's Word to transform our hearts each and every day.

"Pride goes before destruction, and a haughty spirit before a fall." — *Proverbs 16:18*

"When pride comes, then comes disgrace, but with the humble is wisdom." — *Proverbs 11:2*

"Ones Pride will bring him low, but he who is lowly in spirit will obtain honor." — *Proverbs 29:23*

"Everyone who is arrogant in heart is an abomination to the Lord; be assured he will not go unpunished." — *Proverbs 16:5*

The blessings in each verse above are very real; so too are the warnings. I truly believe that there will be pastors and preachers that die and face God's eternal judgment because they never truly surrendered to the Lord Jesus. Their work in ministry served as either simply a job to fund their lives, or as a means to gain notoriety and recognition by men. Simultaneously, I believe there will be a number of smokers and bartenders that enter through those pearly gates by the narrow way. The Gospel is, after all, a matter of the heart. Whether you're a pastor, contractor, electrician, plumber, teacher, fast-food worker, janitor, bartender, or traveling cigar peddler, the state of your heart before Christ Jesus is the single most important hurdle that you will ever have to address. You can't escape it. None of us can. You're either one of His children, or an enemy of God.

You see friends, God created everything we can and cannot see. He had a design, and it was perfect. Yet, when Adam and Eve chose to disobey God in Genesis 3, sin entered the world. The apostle Paul tells us in Romans 5:12

"Therefore, just as sin came into the world through one man, and death through sin, and so death spread to all men because all sinned—"

This sin led the world into a state of brokenness. Every great abomination and atrocity ever conceived in the depraved heart of mankind found its genesis in the garden of Eden when the serpent convinced Adam & Eve that they could be like God. It all began with pride. Thousands of years later, we can see clearly the effects of this sin in the world around us. As we recognize these effects in our own lives, and see our own state of brokenness, we have the opportunity to repent of our sins and believe the Gospel. I hope by now you have a clear understanding of what the Gospel is, but there's never a bad time to revisit it.

The Gospel tells us that because of our sin and brokenness, God came into the world as a man named Jesus. He lived a perfect, sinless life and died a torturous death to pay the price of our sins. Romans 6:23 tells us that "…the wages of sin is death, but the free gift of God is eternal life in Christ Jesus our Lord." Hebrews 9:22 tells us that without the shedding of blood there is no forgiveness of sins. Jesus was this sacrifice. He paid it all on the cross. But He didn't stay there! On the third day, His body began to breathe. He stood up, rolled the massive stone at the entrance of the tomb away and walked out. And just as He was buried and raised to walk again, so each of us has the opportunity to surrender to Him, be buried in His likeness through baptism, and raised to walk in newness of life!

What does this have to do with our pride though? Everything! Alistair Begg connected the Gospel and man's pride quite well.

"And if I don't preach the Gospel to myself all day and every day, then I will find myself beginning to trust myself, trust my experience, which is part of my fallenness as a man. If I take my eyes off the cross, I can then give only lip service to its efficacy while at the same time living as if my salvation depends upon me. And as soon as you go there, it will lead you either to abject despair or a horrible kind of arrogance. And it is only the cross of Christ that deals both with the dreadful depths of despair and the pretentious arrogance of the pride of man…"

I have heard it said by therapists & psychologists that narcissists are incapable of loving another person. They say that narcissists are so consumed with themselves and their own image that "love" as we know it to be, is an impossible concept for them to grasp. While I agree that this is certainly more difficult in the case of full-fledged narcissists, I reject the superfluous bounds of these statements entirely.

It was impossible for a virgin to conceive a child.

I was impossible for Jesus to raise Lazarus.

It was impossible for Him to heal the blind, lame, and lepers.

It was impossible for a man to raise himself from the dead.

But God…

"And you were dead in the trespasses and sins in which you once walked, following the course of this world, following the prince of the power of the air, the spirit that is now at work in the sons of disobedience— among whom we all once lived in the passions of our flesh, carrying out the desires of the body and the mind, and were by nature children of wrath, like the rest of mankind. But God, being rich in mercy, because of the

*great love with which he loved us, even when we were
dead in our trespasses, made us alive together with
Christ—by grace you have been saved— and raised us
up with him and seated us with him in the heavenly
places in Christ Jesus, so that in the coming ages he
might show the immeasurable riches of his grace in
kindness toward us in Christ Jesus. For by grace you
have been saved through faith. And this is not your own
doing; it is the gift of God, not a result of works, so that
no one may boast. For we are his workmanship, created
in Christ Jesus for good works, which God prepared
beforehand, that we should walk in them."*

—   Ephesians 2:1-10

Two of the most beautiful words ever composed by the
Holy Spirit through the hands of men are "But God."
There are no bounds to His power. No limitation to what
He can do in a man's heart. Just as He caused Mary to
give birth, though she was a virgin. Just as He caused
Sarah and Elizabeth to conceive in their old age. Just as
he caused the rotting flesh of Lazarus to come back to
life. Just as He humbled Nebuchadnezzar. Just as He
himself was raised from the dead, so can God almighty
humble the most arrogant of men and restore him to
God's initial design in all humility.

"For nothing will be impossible with God."

—   Luke 1:37

This is the Narcissist Gospel. The greatest, most deceptive sin of all time can be disarmed entirely by the infinite power of God.

Jesus reinforced His divine capability to His disciples when He spoke of the rich entering the Kingdom of Heaven.

'And Jesus said to his disciples, "Truly, I say to you, only with difficulty will a rich person enter the kingdom of heaven. Again I tell you, it is easier for a camel to go through the eye of a needle than for a rich person to enter the kingdom of God." When the disciples heard this, they were greatly astonished, saying, "Who then can be saved?" But Jesus looked at them and said, "With man this is impossible, but with God all things are possible."'

– Matthew 19:23-26

Prior to the Babylonian exile, The Lord had been warning the people of Israel through the prophet Jeremiah of their impending doom, should they not repent of their wicked ways and turn to Him. Yet in this He uttered several words that at the time in their context were fearsome to Jeremiah, however today they are a great comfort to us as His children.

"Behold, I am the Lord, the God of all flesh. Is anything too hard for me?"

– Jeremiah 32:27

This rhetorical question posed by God Almighty serves to reassure us in a number of situations and circumstances that He is indeed God over all. There is nothing too hard for our God. There's nothing that the Omnipotent King of Kings can't accomplish! There exists no mountain that He can't uproot like a freshly sprouted garden weed. Prison walls shatter like tempered glass at His Word.

No matter what our sin be, we need but to turn from them and fix our eyes upon the one who bore them all on the dreadful, bloody cross. He who carried our punishment up Golgotha is the only one that can lift the heavy burden of our pride. But we must first lay it down.

"Through death into life everlasting,

He passed, and we follow Him there;

O'er us sin no more hath dominion,

For more than conquerors we are!

Turn your eyes upon Jesus,

Look full in His wonderful face,

And the things of earth will grow strangely dim,

In the light of His glory and grace."

www.ingramcontent.com/pod-product-compliance
Lightning Source LLC
Chambersburg PA
CBHW071323140726

47996CB00005B/1798